4
278p
2520

D0643382

194   Davidson
P278p   The origins of
D252o   certainty

CHRISTIAN HERITAGE COLLEGE
2100 Greenfield Dr.
El Cajon, CA   92021

The Origins of **Certainty**

The Origins of Certainty

The Origins of **Certainty**
Hugh M. Davidson

Means and Meanings in
Pascal's *Pensées*

The University of Chicago Press
Chicago and London

Hugh M. Davidson is Commonwealth
Professor of French literature at the University
of Virginia. He is the author of *Audience,*
Words, and Art (1965) and coauthor (with P. H.
Dubé) of *A Concordance to Pascal's Pensées*
(1975).

The University of Chicago Press, Chicago 60637
The University of Chicago Press, Ltd., London

© 1979 by The University of Chicago
All rights reserved. Published 1979
Printed in the United States of America
83 82 81 80 79   5 4 3 2 1

Library of Congress Cataloging in Publication Data

Davidson, Hugh McCullough, 1918–
   The origins of certainty.

   Includes bibliographical references and index.
   1. Pascal, Blaise, 1623–1662. Pensées.
2. Apologetics—17th century.   3. Catholic Church—
Doctrinal and controversial works.   4. Certainty.
5. Belief and doubt.   I. Title.
B1901.P43D38   239′.7   78–12768
ISBN 0–226–13716–3

"Nous brûlons du désir de trouver une assiette ferme..." (Fragment 199)

41423

To L. and A.

Contents

Preface

In the following pages I have always started with and usually stayed with the *Pensées* in my attempt to recover and analyze the notion of certainty and its application to belief. Whether engaged in apologetic argument or not, Pascal's thought in the *Pensées* tends as its proper end toward a faith that cannot be doubted.

Most of what I have done here concerns the means to that end: *raison*, *coutume*, and *inspiration*. Chapters 1 and 2 deal with reason, chapter 3 with custom, chapter 4 with inspiration, and chapter 5 summarizes briefly the analysis, broadening the focus somewhat to relate faith to scientific certainty and to suggest some overarching principles in Pascal's way of thinking. I have approached the three main topics by studying the complexes of words, terms, meanings, and designations that surround them. Along with this "nettoyage de la situation verbale" (to borrow Valéry's phrase) I have discussed Pascal's argument in detail. At certain points (notably in chapter 2 and in a general way at the end of chapter 5) it has been possible to establish a matrix or frame of reference that has a great deal to do with fixing the exact meaning not only of the three "moyens de croire," as Pascal calls them, but also of any important term in his thought. The framework functions somewhat like a grid on which words appear in succession like luminous points, their precise value being set by their position at a given moment. Although the image leaves something to be desired, it leads to insight into Pascal's paradoxical and dynamic way of using words.

By this kind of inquiry, not based on comprehensive outlines or *classements* (it does not ignore them entirely) but on a free movement back and forth in the texts and on the idea that the interpreter of the *Pensées* is always to a significant degree *in medias res*, one can put the three original terms into an important sequence. The factors in it interact and converge, however; they are aspects as well as stages of an evolving process. The sequence does not order the fragments either logically or chronologically. The problem, as I have posed it here, is not to fit the pieces of a puzzle together but to provide a standpoint from which to view them, a base from which to start as one tries to see what is in each text and what degree of systematic sense it has. My aim is not to find linear order but to promote intelligibility.

A word about my attitude is perhaps in order. I have sought always to achieve a combination of sympathy and detachment. The former is basic, and I think it will be obvious from the tone of these studies. It does not necessarily entail agreement with Pascal. The more I read him the more sensitive I become to the not infrequent notes of harshness, even of arrogance, and the more I am affected—adversely—by his antimetaphysical prejudices and by the consequent imbalances in his views. But these reservations have nothing to do with my continuing admiration for qualities such as depth, feeling, coherence, inventiveness, brilliance—which stand out on every page. The best way to state my working attitude here may be to say that I have tried to watch and follow Pascal at his work, and to retrieve, at least in part, his habit of language and thought concerning nature, man, and God.

Note

All quotations are taken from the edition of the *Pensées* in three volumes by Louis Lafuma (Paris: Editions du Luxembourg, 1952), and all mentions of fragment numbers refer to that edition.

1 | Proof and Proofs

Certainty and Proof in the Pensées

Pascal puts a high value on certainty in knowledge, and therefore on the search for it and on the ways of reaching it. He sees certainty as a point of repose attained after passing through earlier stages of ignorance or indifference and doubt. In physics and mathematics, reason—discursive reason that works away from intuitive beginnings—is the instrument he uses, both in the discovery and the demonstration of knowledge. Unlimited in those sciences, it must reckon with something radically different in religion. There its status, its characteristic activity, and its proper results all undergo important changes as a consequence of the maxim, "Soumission et usage de la raison, en quoi consiste le vrai christianisme." At a crucial moment it must be silent; it must recognize and accept a light higher than its own or that of any human power. Before and after that moment, when it is active, it does not have as one of its tasks the discovery of religion, since *the* religion is already in view; it focuses its efforts on ways and means of certifying that that religion is divine in origin and true. Moreover, in the *Pensées* Pascal is far less inclined to speak of demonstration than of proof, for the former term has links with geometry and with dogmatism that get in the way of his central argument, though he may use those basically unsuitable connotations heuristically and in passing.

It is my intention here to inquire into the behavior and meaning of the notion of proof in the *Pensées*, when it is seen against the background I have just quickly sketched and when it is watched in the foreground of Pascal's thought. We shall have occasion to note its emergence (and that of some related words) in the fragments, to say how it is defined, to distinguish parts and kinds of proofs, and finally to establish its relative position in a small but important table of ideas.

In a way it is improper to speak as though the *Pensees* form a single undertaking. As any reader of any complete edition knows (I am myself using the Lafuma edition of 1952, in three volumes),[1] these thousand and some odd fragments make up not a text at all, in the usual sense, but, as someone has well said, a pre-text; and to refine the point, one might go on to say that they constitute several pre-texts, with different inner motions and related to different projects.[2] One of these projects is the Apology, visible, of course, in the 382 fragments chosen and grouped into *liasses* by Pascal, but also in many other fragments and notes clearly connected with it, though not included in the author's *classement*. Other projects may be discerned in fragments that seem to belong to the genesis of the *Lettres provinciales*, of the *Ecrits des curés de Paris*, and of an apparently intended *Lettre sur les miracles* (I mention three of the list of suggestions that editors have made with varying degrees of success and consensus). Finally, there is a scattering of *propos* attributed to Pascal, which correspond to no project other than our own desire to preserve as much as possible of what he thought and said.[3]

Without denying or setting aside entirely these diverse intentions, immanent in the texts, I wish to take the *Pensées* here as a single set of data, assuming in them a minimal unity de facto—most of them, by far, concern the Christian religion—but I shall try not so much to study that unity as to bring "proof" and some related terms into a discussion that starts always from particular fragments and moves toward its own unity. This procedure will make it possible for us to leave the topic open for references to other works of Pascal. My main aim is, of course, to contribute something to the understanding of *les Pensées* (let us not forget, though, that Pascal never gave them that title), but on the way we may uncover and define some aspects of *la pensée* of Pascal.

The Place and Parts of Proof

As we approach the subject of proof, we must imagine the situation, the real situation, to which everything Pascal says refers eventually. In the forerank, it includes three essential factors: a prover, a proof or reasoning, and a reader or addressee or interlocutor (as he sometimes becomes when Pascal's dramatic imagination warms up). The real situation has in it, then, a logical aspect that concerns the finding and constructing of proofs, and a psychological and moral aspect that concerns the beliefs and attitudes of the two people. The human aspect is decisive, for logic and reasoning are not ends in themselves, but are adjusted as means to ends that orient human powers. In the second place or rank, as the ultimate points of reference for the discourse, we must add three more factors: men, nature, and the hidden God in whom we are asked to believe.

Now there are three *moyens de croire*, as we are told more than once (as in fragments 808, 821): *raison, coutume*, and *inspiration*. With them in view, the notion of proof and the role it can play emerge with particular clarity. *Preuve* is associated with *esprit*, as something presented to it to which it may open itself. As a first step, that is, one may open one's mind to proofs; and then, in a second step, one may strengthen one's attachment to those proofs by custom or habit, neither of which is strictly speaking a source of proof. Finally, one may offer oneself humbly to *inspirations*, which, again, are not proofs, but they alone bring true conviction.

In fragment 808 Pascal aims to distinguish roles and to be precise in his vocabulary, but in other fragments one notes a certain *flottement*. Custom makes our strongest and most believed proofs (fr. 821); and elsewhere (fr. 149), in a vivid passage where God speaks (as imagined by Pascal), He says that He intends to show men clearly and by "preuves convaincantes" who He is and what He can do. If and when Pascal writes in a literal vein, reason constructs proofs as it goes about its proper discursive activity; and there can be little doubt that this use of terms is basic in his writing and thinking. But he may on occasion broaden his usage and assign "proofs" to the other and nonrational sources of belief. Or he may turn to paradoxes in which all literalness of language is overcome. For example, some Christians *judge by the heart* in matters concerning their faith just as well as those who have knowledge of prophecies and proofs (fr. 382) and can construct arguments on the basis of that knowledge. At one point in the *pari* (fr. 418), Pascal tells his imagined listener: "C'est en manquant de preuve qu'ils [les chrétiens] ne manquent pas de sens." In such instances, where he applies language flexibly, teasing it and making it surprise us, we recognize the symptoms of his dialectical vein. The very absence of proof is a kind of proof, a sign of a superior consistency and reason for certainty.

Pascal appears to see proof as implied in a play of *suppositions* and what may be advanced as suitable *presuppositions*. Since he is not discovering the truth but defending it, he starts logically with suppositions and

moves backward to what they presuppose. (We are re-
minded of the little formula "raison des effets," which occurs frequently in the *Pensées*. It, too, suggests a kind of
analytic procedure that is backward-looking, though the
emphasis seems different—on explanation as opposed to
proof. The "raison" of an "effet" tells why something happens as it does; a proof also tells why, but the stress is on
why something may be said to be so.) Here a curious fact
needs to be noted. We should ordinarily be inclined to say
that a proof is an organism consisting of two parts, an
antecedent and a consequent. However, as Pascal uses the
word, *preuve* refers to the former, the presupposition,
rather than to the latter, to the certifying part rather than to
the whole instance of reasoning. In any case, an antecedent and a consequent are the main elements with which
we must deal. To be quite precise we must also add or
understand a sort of sentence adverb that qualifies the
tightness of the connection between the presupposition
and the supposition. There are very few things that have
been fully proved, such is the weakness of our knowing
powers, and such is, indeed, the intent (as Pascal understands it) of the *Dieu caché*.

Pascal characteristically begins with Nature and
Scripture, with man and God; the proofs we find relate to
these two.[4] Although he sees the possibility of using in
some of his proofs Nature in the sense of physical universe, he limits himself usually to human nature. Reasoning about man and God that starts from the courses of the
moon and the planets he dismisses as being too far removed from men's ordinary way of thinking and as too
complicated ("imbriqué"). That is especially so when the
subject is the existence of God; the argument changes
when we attempt to say something to ourselves about the
nature of God, for the infinites of Nature prefigure Him
and meet in Him. In what follows I should like to give
some sense of the wide range in phrasing—not to say

confusion—that occurs, in fact, with regard to what is supposed and presupposed. To be "proved," then: the greatness of man, God, man, events, the Old Testament, the
New Testament, Jesus Christ, propositions, Christians, divinity, laws and customs, truths, first principles, Moses,
judgments regarding faith, the Christian religion, obscure
things, corruption and redemption, the advantages of the
Jewish people, figures, beliefs, prophecies. And here are
some of the means or presuppositions by which those
items may be proved: the misery of man, Jesus Christ,
nature, prophecy, the Old Testament, the New Testament,
antiquity, clarity, miracles, propositions, the "Machine,"
experience, reason, marvels, absurdities, morality, doctrine, figures. Neither of these lists is complete, nor can
they be neatly correlated. But the many extremely diverse
references to proof and proving and the interesting repeti-
tion of items in the two columns put us in the presence of a
problem. How may this situation be clarified? What elements of order may be found in the way the words and
arguments behave?

Suppositions and Presuppositions

The attempt that I shall make to cover the various cases
involves a certain amount of technical or semitechnical
vocabulary, which I shall rehearse at once; there will be
occasion later to explain and qualify it and, above all, to
show how it applies to a number of particular cases. Let us
begin with the suppositions. They most often are singular,
and can be stated in a single word or phrase, though more
than one *preuve* may be adduced for the support of what
they propose. A point is at issue and needs to be certified.
The difficulty is, however, that the single item (such as
"J.-C. prouvé par les prophéties") usually conceals a proposition. Over and over again we must take the supposition, consisting of a word or phrase, and expand it (at our

risks and perils) if we are to understand what Pascal means. (1) In the instance given, the telescoped proposition proved by the prophecies would no doubt run something like this: "that Jesus Christ is the Messiah." In other words, one large category of suppositions has to do with the nature, the essence, or the identity of something or someone. Sometimes the full statement is given; most often it is not, and we must supply it. (2) Another sizable group of proofs involves attributes rather than natures: instead of defining the thing or person we affirm some predicate of it. "Preuves de Moïse," for example, would seem to be the formula for "Moses as someone whose word can be trusted"; or, if we expand it into a proposition, the result might be: "that Moses tells or told the truth." (3) In a number of other fragments, Pascal deals with the existence of something or someone and, most commonly, with the existence of God. "Preuves de Dieu" means, therefore, that there are available to us or not available to us proofs for affirming "that God exists." (Note, however, that it might fall into category 2 above; then the force of the phrase would be: "that God is the Divine Being.") I am convinced that any discussion of proof soon runs into this phenomenon of the occult statement, and the attempt must be made to penetrate Pascal's shorthand and to bring the hidden elements out into the light. Actually, there is nothing startling or original about this. The categories of essence, attribute, and existence are inevitable; but it is useful to be explicit about them and to recognize, as we shall show in later examples, that the type of the interpreted supposition has consequences for the presupposition and the analytical act of proving. A kind of matching is required. When we undertake to do that, we find that telescopings of the sort just noted are by no means rare in the other part of the typical argument, in the antecedent justification or *preuve*—properly speaking—that Pascal offers us.

In these presuppositions he sometimes presents a single consideration that makes a consequence valid; but one's general impression, which is borne out by a review of the facts, is that Pascal had a head full of proofs, that the whole subject of the Christian religion is surrounded by swarms of proofs waiting to be grasped and put to use. This abundance leads him often to speak of *preuves* in the plural without making any distinctions; at other times he enumerates them or works them into a sequence. In any particular case we have to ask ourselves whether he is using one proof, or several without distinction (tagged by the noun "preuves" used collectively), or several forming a list or series. And, again, he sets himself tasks of very different scope, according to whether he turns his mind to his enterprise as a whole and the entire process that is designed to bring his reader to a positive, faith-seeking posture (then we have "preuves de la religion chrétienne"), or whether he directs his attention to this or that point on the way. He can run swiftly through all the *moyens de croire* to back up Christianity as a single presupposition, or he can stop and linger over details, adjusting his proof to the difficulty at hand—an obscure prophecy in the Old Testament, a difficult passage in the New, a paradoxical bit of human behavior.

Species of Proofs

These technical distinctions allow us to discern numbers and categories of assertions. They are certainly applicable and are even inevitable in the study of Pascal's proofs, as we approach them from outside and above, so to speak. We move on to more interesting indications of patterns of thought that are familiar to him (and perhaps unconscious) when we try to define species of proof that occur in the *Pensées* and to recover their distinctive principles. After all, there are different kinds as well as degrees of certainty, and this consideration must have implications for what Pascal wishes to do. The facts show that although he is ready to *faire flèche de tout bois*, and does so more than once, so that a complete spectrum of proving activities appear in the *Pensées*, he has nonetheless his favorites, and they give us a valuable glimpse of deeply set logical tendencies.

Let us look at a few examples and their characteristic traits. In a long variant (fr. 109) Pascal discusses the question of motion or change in things as the Pyrrhonians might do. He says that we as individuals see things moving and changing; we utter the same words about them. But do we conceive them in the same way? Do we have the same ideas about what is happening? There appears the *supposition*: that we do agree in our conceptions. What is the *presupposition*? We have only a strong conjecture, based on a habit of language—on a kind of custom. But at least we have that, and it constitutes one species of proof recognized by Pascal: proof that is pragmatic or operational. What we do *not* have is a presupposition stating that the terms we use in the presence of moving things have the clarity, the fixed meanings, the absence of ambiguity that would be found in mathematical discourse. And so, by the contrast shown in this first example, which is skeptical in tone but also critical of skepticism, we may distinguish two lines of proof, two kinds of statement that Pascal can accept as certain and probative: those based on habit and those based on geometrical procedure. (Already in fragment 7, near the beginning of the so-called *papiers classés*,[5] he has spoken of "preuves par la machine" in a clear reference to the kind of proof or validation that arises from habit.)

In fragment 110 we note a shift from a concern with proof to a concern with proofs. We are looking for something plural that will explain the first principles of rational or scientific knowledge. Again the results of Pascal's reflections turn out to be negative, but no matter, the example reveals once more what is required in a certain kind of proving activity. The suppositions in this instance are assertions about existence: there *is* such a thing as space, as time, as movement, as numbers. Scientific reason accepts these principles and works with them. From what starting point or points may it infer that they are true? The answer is that it cannot in fact provide proofs for these principles. If they have any certainty, it comes from the heart, which feels or senses them immediately. This fragment reminds us of the necessity, for anyone who tries to understand Pascal's thought, of realizing that for him what the heart knows intuitively to be true lies beyond the grasp of reason. But that is another discussion. If we take the context here to be discursive knowing and concentrate on the role of these "principles," I think it fair to say that, as Pascal uncovers the sentimental origins of rational certainty, he gives us another sketch of the geometrical kind of proof, where reason, moving from definitions, axioms, and other propositions, arrives at theorems which are consequents, that is, suppositions.

In fragment 122, the topic is the "condition de l'homme." Wretchedness ("misère"), we are told, is a proof of greatness ("grandeur") and vice versa. Each of these suppositions—here present in their occult or telescoped forms—may be drawn or concluded from the other (Pascal's verbs are forms of *tirer* and *conclure*). We start here on a new line of proving, the most important of all, the one along which Pascal travels in pulling together the whole of his religious and theological reflection. The turn of the argument is typically dialectical. One of the commonest features of such reasoning is the tendency to pose and overcome distinctions. That is the leading impulse here. By nature and in fact (attribute and existence are thus made to coincide) man is wretched and man is great (two contradictory assertions are thus both true); and either may serve as the antecedent that proves the other (a supposition may thus be also a presupposition). Once you have affirmed definitely and with conviction one of the items in these linked pairs, you have affirmed the other. This type of argument, with the frequent inversions it allows, differs markedly from what we have seen in the instances or adumbrations of "customary" and "geometrical" proofs. Pascal is now seeking the origin of certainty elsewhere.

In fragment 137 the topic is distractions ("divertissements"). What Pascal thinks is true, his supposition (as I have been calling it, generalizing slightly his own vocabulary), is stated without indirection of any kind: "Un roi sans divertissement est un homme plein de misères." He does say that he is not thinking of Christian kings insofar as they are Christian; the implication is, though, that there are not enough kings Christian enough to affect the argument. On what grounds (that is, proofs) does he feel that he may declare such a thing so confidently? Put the point to the test, he says; leave your king without his amusements, without company, without any external concern, without any satisfaction of his senses, but with time to think about himself; and then the assertion will be verified. This time Pascal proposes to our attention something that looks like a little experiment, a little study of the covariation of elements in a controlled situation. The predicate will be established inductively, as we might be tempted to say at first. But this is really a reasoning about cause and effect that belongs finally in the syllogistic mode, although it is experimental in appearance. The absence of *divertissement* is the middle term that serves to link the subject and predicate in the statement. Every man without distraction is miserable, and if a king comes in the scope of the subject term of the major premise, he must take the consequence and be "plein de misères." In regular language and form it might go like this: every man without distraction is miserable; some king (even) is without distraction; and such a king is miserable.

Four types of proofs have emerged, then, in these early fragments. I am persuaded that they are the fundamental types for Pascal, and that in one guise or another, sometimes in mixtures or combinations, they give us the keys to his way of thinking when he sets out to prove something.[6] A given affirmation may be certified or at least partially certified by reasoning that involves: (1) processes of composition *more geometrico*, where y is justified by x because it follows from and takes its place in an orderly series based on x; (2) processes of definition and inspection, where y is justified by x because it meets the conditions laid down in x; (3) processes of conflict and resolution, where y is justified by x, because x implies y as its opposite, or where y, which embodies a contradiction, is justified or rendered intelligible by x because x introduces the means of removing the contradiction; (4) processes of discernment, where y is justified by x because x makes explicit what happened in y or, on occasion, what factor caused y to happen.[7] In the *Pensées* there are many examples of 2, 3, and 4; a few of type 1 (that I have been able to find). The best way to make clear what is involved in this general classification of proofs is, I think, to run through some further examples, under each heading, starting with the first, less richly furnished group. (There is a reason for this scantiness if one stops to think that, as Pascal observes—and no doubt rightly—the *esprit géométrique* is technical. In its usual working it requires us to turn our eyes from the people and things surrounding us, from common experience to the properties of ideal numbers, lines, and figures. It requires such powers of concentration, abstraction, and sustained attention that an Apology of the Christian religion based on some transposition of these requirements would limit its audience severely from the outset. Besides, Saint Paul and Saint Augustine do not use this technique.)

Examples of Geometrical Proofs

In fragment 382 Pascal evokes two sets of people who are without *preuves* and cannot back up what they say, even though they may say it with assurance: infidels and heretics on the one hand, and certain convinced Christians on the other. Their terms, their propositions are similar, and it looks like an even match that cannot be settled by argumentation, for these Christians judge by the heart and through divine inspiration, rather than by the head and reason. To be proved, then, is that these Christians are right and the others wrong. Now there are other Christians who know the prophecies and the proofs, and they can demonstrate without difficulty that these Christians of the heart are truly inspired by God. This example gives us only a fleeting glimpse of the logical impulse I wish to illustrate, but it does not miss the mark completely, in that Pascal assumes the possibility of a formal comparison of terms and propositions, some of which have the self-evidence of axioms, and also in that he refers in the passage to Christians who have the kind of triumphant confidence that goes with power to demonstrate in the geometrical mode.

The passage reminds one of the "Cela est démonstratif, etc." that concludes the calculations of the *pari*, just before Pascal and his interlocutor turn to the subject of the passions and moral discipline. The fragment is, of course, number 418, and the reasoning before that pivotal point falls very clearly in the category of proof conceived in the mode of *composition*, as I am here using that word. To be proved: that thinking along a line that presupposes the existence of God is not an offense to reason. Pascal performs first a crucial act of assimilation, by changing a problem of theology into a problem of applied mathematics; he then assembles, step by step, case by case, a long argument in which moral realities move about like terms in algebra, and lives and attitudes become finite stakes to bet or not on finite or infinite gains, with very unfavorable or very favorable odds and with varying degrees of certainty (he quantifies the mental state itself!). In all this we have a pure example of the kind of analysis and synthesis, sequentially done and carried rigorously to a conclusion, that characterizes the type of proof that is based on a geometrical model.

Examples of Syllogistic Proofs

The second line of thinking that is probative or convincing for Pascal depends on insight, definition, judgment, and discursive movement; it suggests the distinctions and procedures of traditional logic. In fragment 190 he takes up the metaphysical proofs of God ("les preuves de Dieu métaphysiques"). To understand what he is getting at, we must first expand the phrase "preuves de Dieu", as it is undoubtedly one of those latent propositions of which I spoke earlier. It means, in shorthand, the proofs of God as an existent Being, or in propositional form, the proofs to the effect that God exists. With this in mind we may examine some of the technical aspects of this example. Its force is essentially negative; it tells us what proofs are not really effective, though for some they may serve briefly. These metaphysical grounds for asserting that God exists have two fatal weaknesses: they are complicated, and they are far removed from the ordinary way men reason. (We meet again, apropos of these proofs and more explicitly than before, the objection we saw in connection with the geometrical ones.) They may be valid for a short while, as long as one has the proof in mind, but the conviction does not last; and they are really satisfying only to those who come to them with some faith or persuasion already. The structure of this example belongs to the logic of syllogism. The assertion that metaphysical proofs are of little utility is validated by an appeal to the traits (1) of nearness to common ways of thinking and (2) of simplicity. They would

provide the nexus for an argument in favor of God's existence by serving as the needed middle term between the
subject term (a particular proof) and the predicate (the idea
of lasting utility). The presence or absence of the two
favorable traits causes reasoning to succeed or to fail.
Metaphysical proofs fail because they do not embody
either of these essential qualities. In fragment 781 a similar
proof is presented, tending to show that the truth of "our
religion" is not well proved by studying the courses of the
moon and planets.

This sort of reasoning gravitates toward questions of the
existence, nature, and attributes of men or God or of some
more abstract object of attention, such as the Christian religion.[8] Fragments 389 and 502 offer good examples of the
attempt to establish the nature of what or rather of whom
one is talking about. Pascal asks in fragment 389 why
Christ did not come in a visible and obvious way, instead
of deriving His proof ("tirer sa preuve") from prophecies.
And one might similarly phrase as a question the issue
raised in fragment 502: how can a hidden sense, like that
found in prophetic figures, serve as a proof of the Messiah?
It is useful again in these examples to expand Pascal's shorthand. The thing to be proved is the essential nature of
Jesus, in other words, that He is indeed the Messiah. In
theory the presupposition that underlies this may run
along one of two lines. (1) It may list the visible and unmistakable signs that would define the anointed one; and then
the presence of these signs in a subject would serve to
connect the subject and the predicate. Or, (2) it may seek
hidden and indirect indications that will serve the same
logical function. In fact, the latter is the route Pascal takes.
Without answering at once his own question, the one with
which he begins in fragment 389, he affirms that the distinguishing notes or marks needed to identify a certain
person as the Messiah are present in the Bible as obscure
but effective hints.

If one wishes to extend this argument and say why the

proof did take the form it assumed, one would come back
to the central theme of search and of the requirement that
man must make an effort. The better way to the hidden
God is by spiritual cooperation and by the figurative, indirect sense rather than by enforced obedience. The quality
of the relationship between God and man becomes more
worthy if we take our part of the initiative and seek the
One who is seeking us. Once more we have reasoned with
three terms along the lines of formal logic. This way, since
it requires effort, is the better way.

In the third paragraph of fragment 489 we read, printed
on a line by itself and in capital letters, this formula:
"PROPHÉTIES PREUVE DE DIVINITÉ." The context makes it
possible to recover what the word "divinité" refers to and
what the statement or affirmation is that Pascal intends by
this single term. The argument as a whole amounts to this:
"I, the God of the Jewish people, am the real God, the one
who is truly divine. Why is that so? Because through those
who speak for me, my prophets, it is clear that I have that
knowledge of origins, of things past, and of things to come
that is an essential characteristic of Divinity." All sages
who oppose these prophets and all gods who oppose this
one may be measured by the standard of unlimited knowledge. The presence or absence of this middle term determines whether the predicate "divine" is legitimate or not.
Obviously this instance of proof belongs also to the syllogistic category. It reaches a conclusion that is validated
by reference to an "essential" definition.

It is easy to find cases where Pascal uses the same technique of proof in judgments that affirm attributes rather
than essential natures. Fragment 292 concerns the veracity
of Moses. Can we say with confidence that Moses tells the
truth? On the answer to this question hangs the value of a
very important part of the Bible. Pascal constructs his
argument in terms of the way in which truth may become
altered and corrupted. That happens when it must pass

over a long line of generations. But lives were long and generations were relatively few from the Creation to (say) the Deluge, and so the contents of Mosaic books had little time to deteriorate; thus they meet this standard of veracity: they are proved. In another example that denies rather than affirms a supposition Pascal refers twice (in frs. 310 and 457) to the hypothesis of the deceiving apostles ("les apôtres fourbes"). According to this view the biblical accounts of the gospel are the fruit of a plot instigated by the apostles, who invented them, launched them, and then upheld them consistently. This hypothesis is false—"absurde" is Pascal's word for it—because of the weakness of human nature. To bring down the whole plot, the weakness of only one of the twelve would have sufficed; something he would have let slip would have shown up the deception of all. There is a syllogistic turn to this: no man can escape the possibility of indiscretion; the apostles were men; therefore they were weak, too weak to keep a secret. Although Pascal does not himself go so far, it seems that a nice paradox results, in that weak and indiscreet men are likely to tell the truth!

Finally, as an instance of the same way of reasoning on a theme that appears often in the *Pensées*, I should like to mention fragment 454. There Pascal compares religions and isolates the marks that make one more worthy of attention than another. He thinks he has an indubitable way of showing the special standing of the Christian religion. There have been many inventors of religions ("faiseurs de religions"); he mentions the Romans, the Egyptians, the Chinese, the Mohammedans. As the first step in his argument, he notes that they lack adequate moral teaching and proofs: "ils n'ont ni la morale qui peut me plaire, ni les preuves qui peuvent m'arrêter." However, in the second stage of the argument (repeating in a subtler way the same procedure, which consists in locating the marks or notes that will serve to justify affirmations or negations about subjects), he goes back to something deeper even than proofs by morality and by miracles, to what he calls "fondements," a term clearly belonging in the same order of ideas as the word "preuve." It has historical overtones, since his topic is inventors of religions. A look at the Jewish people, its history, its law, its promises, and its claims suffices to convince us that we cannot ignore it. Because of these points the Jews stand out when compared with the other religious traditions mentioned; they fulfill the conditions required for being a people worthy of special attention. This kind of argument occurs in many places, especially in connection with the word "marque": Pascal discovers and repeats various marks singly or in groups that serve as proofs of the special status—and indeed of the truth—of Christian religion.

Examples of Dialectical Proofs

A third way of reasoning and proving presents itself when Pascal uses the devices of dialectic. In our logical tradition there have been several species of dialectic and different positions regarding its status and proper use (it clearly does not have the same meaning and value for Plato and Aristotle or Kant and Hegel), but it is not impossible to discern in its various forms some features that appear to be essential. All of them show a concern for multiplicity and unity, for tensions or conflicts that call for resolution. There seem to be two characteristic phases or movements: (1) apparent unity at the beginning of the discussion tends, on further inspection, to dissolve into opposition, conflict, and controversy; and (2) apparent contradiction turns out to be capable of resolution, of statement in some way that unifies all opposed terms or views. The first of these is normally the initial phase; but it may be impossible to go beyond it, and the dialectic may come to an uneasy rest in unavoidable diversity. The second phase is usually terminal, but in pure and truly open-ended dialectic the discussion is always subject to reconsideration, and what was thought to be *res judicata* may become the point of departure for identifying new differences or contraries, and the process starts over again. A proof in such a line of thought is anything that causes movement in either the initial and negative phase or the terminal and positive phase. In other words, anything that forces us to recognize a contradiction or shows us the way to a reconciliation functions as a proof.

There is reason to believe, as I have said elsewhere, that this mode of thinking is the primary one in the *Pensées* of Pascal.[9] It lies behind great blocks of his reasoning, such as the one that depends on the notion of "l'homme sans Dieu" and the corresponding one that follows from the idea of "l'homme avec Dieu"; it works itself out likewise in the table of the three orders (of bodies, minds, and hearts); and without those two sets of distinctions and the context defined by them the leading argument of the fragments cannot be constituted. Here my intention is to show that other modes of thinking are present in the *Pensées*, though one must add, I think, that they are subordinated to the general logical outline, which remains dialectical. In this section what concerns us is a dialectic on a microscopic scale, dialectic as it occurs where Pascal presents individual proofs, rather than in principles that serve to integrate the *Pensées* as a whole (insofar as one may speak of the fragments and *liasses* as forming a whole). For we do in fact see the common features of this kind of reasoning at work in very specific guises. There are many particular *preuves* that have at the origin of their force this logical tendency, which Pascal accepts as being axiomatically valid, just as he accepts the compositional and reflexive or syllogistic devices without question. As before, it will be necessary, in most cases, to make explicit by expansion from Pascal's short formulas the conclusion to be proved, before the line of proof can be established.

In fragment 199, for example, sometimes referred to as

"Les Deux infinis" but better understood if we keep the title set by Pascal, "Disproportion de l'homme," there comes a point at which he wishes to consummate the proof of our human weakness by reflections on nature.[10] The proposition to be proved becomes then, that man is weak; and the proof consists in bringing vividly into view the antithetical term of strength-and-greatness, which is applied to nature. Nature is unlimited and durable, whereas man is finite and ephemeral. Pascal brings us face to face with an enormous inequality or disproportion. Clearly we are in the negative phase of the argument, which, after stunning us with some vertiginous ideas and imagery, leaves us at the end in an uncomfortable, unresolved tension. We see another example of the same sort in fragments 305 and 311 (especially in the latter). Pascal develops there what he calls "les preuves de Jésus-Christ." He means proofs that make it legitimate, or at the very least, intelligible, to assert that Jesus was and is the Messiah. Again, the tactic is to evoke an impressive counterterm—the Jews, and their scattering and misfortunes. Their fate stems from the original prophecies that they would not recognize the Messiah and that they would be captives. The two sides of this argument imply each other, so that if one side is posed, the other comes automatically into sight. With the coming of the Messiah the Jews will be in a certain state; with the Jews in a certain state, the Messiah has come. In fragment 501, we may discern still another example of this tendency to use a contradiction as a means of making a proposition acceptable, as a means of proving it. Here there is no need to expand a formula. Pascal states from the outset the complete proposition: "que l'Ancien Testament n'est que figuratif." As he reads the prophets, they said contradictory things about good and evil, man and God; and they said, in addition, that they would not be understood, that what they uttered contained a hidden sense, spiritual and not simply temporal. Thus the Old Testament contains statements that seem to destroy each other. Here we note that the supposition according to which the Old Testament is figurative calls for a presupposition in which conflicting prophecies and senses are posed. There is no way to go on to the notion of *figure* without that preliminary analysis. This complex example poses contradiction on the level of prophecies in order to legitimize a further opposition, that between confusion based on those prophecies and clarity based on figures. It is on the borderline between the positive and negative phases of Pascal's line of reasoning, since figurative interpretation is a source or principle of unity. There is mutual implication in both stages of the proof: one prophecy requires another prophecy to produce contradiction; and prophecies require figures and their double meanings to produce consistency. (We have not yet reached the moment at which it becomes clear that the figures will make it possible to resolve the even more important contradiction between the two great blocks of the Bible—the Old and New Testaments—so that the two may be seen to constitute a single account.)

Another phase of the dialectic appears in fragment 309. Pascal says that Jesus Christ said great things so simply as to make one believe he had not thought them out, but so clearly as to show that he knew very well what he was saying. Such naïveté combined with such clarity is admirable; taken together they make up one of the "Preuves de J.-C." I mean one of the proofs of *Jesus Christ as divine*, for this would seem to be the correct way to expand Pascal's thought here. The two opposed qualities, when found together as predicates indicate an extraordinary subject—a divine person. This example will serve to introduce others having the same basic form. An apparently irreconcilable opposition shows itself to be capable of resolution in a single term or person or reality, and, since it contains the elements needed for the synthesis, it serves as the antecedent that "proves" the synthesis. In fragment 418, at the beginning of the analysis that sets forth the odds, the stakes, and the possible rewards of the man who bets on the existence of God, the skeptical interlocutor questions the stand of convinced Christians. Lacking proof, they should have taken no stand on the alternative that God does or does not exist. Pascal wants to show that the Christians are not inconsistent in their conviction; and he does so by a paradox, which supplies out of itself the force of the proof. On the one hand Christians have no final, rational proof for what they believe, nor do they make any such claim. They know that their wisdom is folly, *stultitia*, and based on faith. It is by lacking proof and by bearing witness to a superior source of certainty that they attain consistency. Their situation is contradictory, but their strength arises precisely from a grasp of that contradiction.

We find other examples of this sort of reconciliation in fragments 449 and 431. In the first of these we are told that, if the world existed in order to teach man about God, the divinity of God would be obvious on every hand. What we actually see in the world, however, is proof of these two affirmations: the corruption and the redemption of man. They are opposed but complementary truths that make sense only when we recognize that the world exists by and for Jesus Christ. In Him is seen the sense of the two truths and the partiality of either taken by itself. Corruption and redemption both point to Jesus Christ, and because of that He "proves" them. The two opposed truths may also be taken as items to be proved separately. This occurs in fragment 431. The two proofs are drawn, respectively, from the impious, characterized by their indifference to Christian religion, and from the Jews, characterized by their irreconcilable opposition to that religion. Pascal takes this indifference as understandable only with reference to the faithful, and consequently as in some way monstrous, corrupt; he takes the enmity and opposition as understandable only with reference to Jesus Christ as the Messiah. In other words, in this complex logical figure, indifference and enmity (already two opposed terms) each bears witness—by opposition—to the two essential truths (also opposed) of corruption and redemption. These antithetical elements that imply each other can enter ipso facto into a set of premises that is synthetic and true. For in a well-stated contradiction each side evokes or proves the other, and together they open the way to a third term (here Jesus Christ) that by its harmonizing function proves both itself and the original antithesis.

In fragment 502 we return to a simpler, more clear-cut example. In order to serve as proof of the Messiah, that is, as proof of the assertion that Jesus Christ is the Messiah, the sense of the Bible must be hidden, but not too hidden. A mixture of obscurity and clarity is what is needed. If the spiritual sense were entirely clear, those whose lives center in the flesh would not be able to keep and bear it; if it were entirely hidden, no one would have access to it; but thanks to a revelation or sense that is partly equivocal and partly univocal, we (or some of us) have the means of proving the spirituality of Christ and his status as the Messiah.

Examples of Pragmatic Proofs

A fourth line of proof-seeking thought in the *Pensées* remains to be noted. In this last perspective, certainty has its origin in some effective cause or agent. The proof depends on authority, on a prophet's gift, or on God's power. With this topic we inevitably move into a diverse lot of questions concerning miracles or external signs of divine power, inclinations due to the action of God in individual hearts, and—not to neglect a lower but very potent force in proof—the works of *la Machine*. But prophecy furnishes the best examples. It gets a great deal of attention in the *Pensées*; it is the "greatest of all proofs of Jesus Christ"; it makes possible a unified view of the two testaments; and as a theme it introduces and sums up a whole side of Pascal's argument: PROPHÉTIES PREUVE DE DIVINITÉ.

Often one must, I think, recognize in the treatment of

prophecy a blending of dialectic and what I shall call a dramatic or pragmatic kind of proving activity. Any prophecy includes two elements, the prophetic utterance or prediction and the accomplishment that occurs later. Of course the two parts are very closely bound together, so that we may easily slip into the dialectical situation where two terms or elements imply each other immediately. In outline form, the reasoning runs like this. We can see that something is true of y now in view of something said long ago by x. A coherent account results when the two pieces of the puzzle are put together, each piece validating the other. Thus in fragments 189, 240, 335, and 819 Jesus Christ is proved—as Messiah—by the prophecies; they constitute "preuves solides et palpables" (fr. 189). For us there is something odd about this, because we tend, I think, to approach such a question as though the prediction were a kind of hypothesis, and our habit is to say that the prediction is confirmed by the event. Pascal sees it, most often, just the other way around. The prophecies prove, confirm, certify the event. He does write in fragment 939 that to understand the prophecies one must await their accomplishment, the time when the things predicted have taken place, which seems more in keeping with the idea of prophecy as a species of hypothesis. However, it is probably a mistake to insist on that way of interpreting the fragment. The sort of alternating current of validation that Pascal discovers here is more likely another instance of the behavior of terms in a dialectic.

The matter cannot rest here, however. Prophecy has an effective causal influence on the course of events; the problem is not simply one of finding coherence and mutual intelligibility. We have a prophetic statement made at one moment in time and in one set of circumstances that is followed by a correlative event at a later time in another set of circumstances. The context is one of narration and history rather than of logic and logical relationships. Pascal draws our attention to the particular people who make these utterances, insisting on the need to distinguish the false from the true prophets, and when the alleged realization of the prophecy is before us, we must again weigh evidence and make discerning judgments. This kind of sensitivity and this emphasis on people and facts are characteristic of reasoning that is circumstantial and pragmatic. Tracing events back to an authoritative agent differs from anything we have seen before. It is not like tracing a conclusion back to a structure of terms and propositions that guarantees it, or attempting to locate in a subject essential aspects that may serve as the means of reasonings, or setting up contradictions, paradoxes, and syntheses.

Actually, in studying how this dramatic line of thought works in connection with prophecy, one discovers two steps. The first shows once more how the various modes of proof reinforce each other in Pascal's mind. (1) When he says that prophecies are proofs of divinity, the argument is, that to know what is to come, and to prophesy it, and to make it happen—all these are clearly beyond human capabilities. Consequently, to be able to do such a thing belongs to God and, through him, to a few favored individuals, his prophets. This moment in the proof is syllogistic in character. (2) With that general conclusion established—that true prophecy belongs to God—any prophecy that is realized becomes part of the divine plan. This means that the accomplishments of all the prophecies concerning the Messiah and the conclusion that Jesus is the Christ are warranted by the fact of prophecy and by the supernatural agent standing behind prophecy.[11]

One sees this sort of "preuve de J.-C." in fragments 189, 240, 335, and 819 (to mention only a few examples). In all these the thesis that the promised Savior came is established by attaching that event to the will and power of God, who speaks by the prophets. But prophecy has still another application as the guarantor of a crucial conclusion concerning the Bible. Pascal asserts, in fragment 274, that both Testaments are proved at once by the realization of prophecy. He means that, thanks to the force of prophecy, the two Testaments, when put together, give a coherent, unified, and true report of facts. Once more we must be aware of the parallel working of the dialectical and pragmatic lines of proof. *Prophecies* form one of the terms of a dialectically related pair, the other being *realizations* (we are in the realm of thought, not of time and history); they are also factors in the sequence of human events, as antecedents that lead to consequents (we are in the realm of existence and history). They are decisive in either perspective. Without them the logical and causal relationships between the two Testaments evaporate, mutual implication and continuity disappear, and revelation falls apart. Prophecies, as manifestations of divine wisdom and power, justify what we say about the two great divisions of the Bible, and what we say about the nature of Christ, and in part, at least, what we say about divinity itself.

In the category of pragmatic or dramatic thinking there is something new in Pascal's proofs. He has taken us more or less clearly out of the domain of rational, man-made proofs and sources of certainty into two new territories, one above and the other below reason. (1) There are proofs by inspiration and infused conviction or by miracles. Because of the proportions assumed by these two notions in the *Pensées*, it seems best to treat them separately and at greater length in a later chapter. Let it suffice to say here that, in their function as proofs, miracles (like prophecies) require the intervention of God in the normal order of things. The difference is that miracles are not usually foretold, and correlation with past saying is less important than relevance to a present situation, to an immediate crisis that calls for a remedy or a doctrine that needs spectacular confirmation. (2) The last source of certainty—one that lies, again, essentially outside the works of reason—is what Pascal calls "la

Machine," a term associated with the body and with habit. In fragment 418, for example, at the end of the demonstrative part of the *pari*, he tells his interlocutor that instead of continuing along the line of adding to the "preuves de Dieu," the next step or aim is to diminish the passions. In other words, after reaching a certain point in intellectual progress toward faith, we must turn our attention to moral progress. Use the Machine; act *as if* you believe; form a habit—such advice shows on Pascal's part a willingness to accept proofs that are judged less by the light of reason than by their effectiveness. Action by habit does as a matter of fact strengthen inchoate belief, and that is justification enough. Indeed, in fragment 821, where we learn we are "automate autant qu'esprit," the action of habit ("coutume") is alleged to make the strongest and most convincing proofs. With this fourth species of certainty, based on what I have called pragmatic or dramatic means, we complete, I believe, the list of kinds of proofs that appear in the *Pensées*. They may be correlated with the three seats or starting points of proof in man, as Pascal conceives him: mind, heart, and body. From mind and its characteristic motions we derive proofs by recomposing in geometrical fashion the results of analysis, by judging in the light of definitions, and by uniting oppositions. From the heart and the body we derive proofs by noting the effects of active causes, either spiritual or mechanical.[12]

Short Sequences of Proofs

In all the examples discussed so far the reasoning is composed of two elements: the supposition, which is to be justified or certified or proved, and a presupposition that serves to establish that primary part. I think most of the *preuves* in the *Pensées* consist of these relatively isolated pairs of terms (or propositions, when terms are expanded so as to fix the exact sense of the inference). There is a rhetorical advantage in this form, since the reader grasps it with a minimum of bother and without having to keep in mind a chain of reasons. I have found, however, two interesting examples of compound forms, where Pascal arranges more than two elements into longer patterns of proof.

In fragment 189 he writes that God is known to us and proved to us only by Jesus Christ, and Jesus Christ is proved, in turn, by the prophecies (those "preuves solides et palpables"), and the prophecies are proved finally by the fact of having been fulfilled. If we take up these affirmations one by one, we find that this instance of reasoning is not only compound in the sense I have indicated but also interesting in that more than one type of proof comes into play. (1) Insofar as God is concerned, this fragment proves not His existence but His accessibility. Pascal is speaking of Him as available to man, in spite of the gulf that separates the divine from the human. The proof consists in finding and posing a third term, Jesus Christ, between the two sides of this antithesis. In Him and through Him we know God; without Him (that is, without Scripture and what it teaches about original sin, and a necessary mediator who was promised and sent) we cannot prove God absolutely. Among the four types of proof that I have defined, this belongs clearly to dialectic, since its virtue is based on locating the means of overcoming an opposition. To find the harmonizing factor in such a case is to establish a certainty based on coherence and unity. (2) Pascal's mind moves on to Jesus Christ: on the basis of what may we assert Him? What is to be proved is Jesus as the Messiah, that is, that He is the Messiah. For proving Him we have the contents of the prophecies. Among the kinds of proof I have distinguished this appears to be, in a shortened form, an example of inference based on traits and essential conditions. The identity of Christ as the promised redeemer is guaranteed by the fact of correspondence between what was prophesied about the Messiah and what He was and did. This is mediation, if you will, but in a sense different from that of the preceding example. Here it occurs in the classical form of a middle term and an implied syllogism, and the reasoning is logical rather than dialectical. (3) In turn, we may ask, what warrant have we for the prophecies? Here we enter on a third line of thought, which is permeated by the dimension of time and the notion of events occurring in succession. Words offered as prophetic are borne out by what happens; and that implies an extraordinary authority behind the words spoken— nothing less than the authority of God. And so we come again to the last of the type of proofs, in which our certainty arises from the presence of divine capability and action. In this part of the compound we have an example of the dramatic or instrumental kind of thinking and reasoning.

Fragment 274 contains another striking illustration of the way in which separate proofs or segments may be combined to form a chain, with variations in the kind of certainty at each step. The fragment begins with a kind of title: "Preuves des deux testaments à la fois." A fair restatement of the reasoning would run as follows: (1) The two Testaments are true, because the prophecies made in one are realized in the other. This argues from words to their consequences in facts and history; it is cast in the pragmatic style of proof. (2) The prophecies have been accomplished, because they have two senses. This step—the identification of two senses—prepares one term of an opposed pair for logical bonding to the other; it harmonizes a discord without suppressing either contrasting element. It takes its place, therefore, in the dialectical mode. (3) The Old Testament texts, the prophecies themselves, have two senses, because of what you find if you study Scripture itself and expecially the proofs given by Rabbis and by the *Cabale*. Pascal lists, without developing them, five (or six if you

allow the variant) written sources of proofs. This phase of
the reasoning, by its appeal to authority returns us to matters of fact and the line of thought noted in (1) above.

Two Lists

Interlocking series of proofs are not very long and are few
in number. By far most of the proofs are discrete acts of the
mind, single, significant acts of linking a supposition to its
presupposition. Pascal *states* proofs, and on rare occasions
he *connects* them explicitly. At two important points, he
enumerates proofs. What he does in these lists is to tell us
without going into details what headings or topics proofs
may come from or be reduced to. In fragment 402, under
the title "Preuves de la religion," he writes, "Morale./
Doctrine./Miracles./Prophéties./Figures." That is all. Obviously we are looking at essential terms or ideas; all of
them have figured in the preceding analyses.

Two comments may be made here. In the first place,
these headings appear to stem mainly from the Scripture
side of the distinction Pascal makes early in the Apology
(in fr. 6), where nature is to supply the proofs of man's
corruption and Scripture will do the same in establishing
the counterthesis, that there is a redeemer. In the second
place, these headings, if one examines them in pairs and in
a linear fashion, seem to have logical relations to each other
and to fall into a kind of sequence. They are not simply
isolated topics. *Morale*, which has to do with practice and
conduct, follows from *doctrine*, which is a matter of theory
or explanation. (As we shall see below in fragment 482,
Pascal's second list of proofs, "doctrine" suggests to Pascal
at once this development: "qui rend raison de tout.")
From this correlation we move to the pair *doctrine/
miracles*, and note once more a close relationship, for one
function of the latter is to justify the former; more than
once Pascal affirms that miracles confirm doctrines and not

vice versa. In turn, *miracles* and *prophéties* have a special connection, for a prophecy is, strictly speaking, the announcement of a miracle; and a miracle, though extraordinary in its own right, becomes all the more so when predicted. Finally, *prophéties* depend on *figures*, for without the double sense that figurative interpretation provides, one cannot establish that the prophecy has in fact been realized. This list faces, therefore, in two directions, upward toward one of the two basic sources of proofs (Scripture), and downward toward particular passages in the *Pensées* where proofs become explicit; and in the relationships of dependence that bind these five terms together as suppositions and presuppositions we are looking, I think, at some of the original impulses from which the various types of proofs are derived.

In fragment 482 Pascal gives a more detailed and more complete list of proofs. Under the single word "PREUVES," he sets down twelve topics:

> 1° La religion chrétienne, par son établissement, par elle-même établie si fortement, si doucement, étant si contraire à la nature.—2° La sainteté, la hauteur et l'humilité d'une âme chrétienne.—3° Les merveilles de l'Ecriture sainte.—4° Jésus-Christ en particulier.—5° Les apôtres en particulier.—6° Moïse et les prophètes en particulier.—7° Le peuple juif.—8° Les prophéties.— 9° La perpétuité: nulle religion n'a la perpétuité.—10° La doctrine, qui rend raison de tout.—11° La sainteté de cette loi.—12° Par la conduite du monde.

This list serves as a commentary on the preceding one.[13] I shall not attempt here any force fitting, but I think one may see that these principles also point upward to the fundamental distinction between nature and Scripture, with Scripture getting far more attention than nature. But there is a clear reference to nature in the first item, and the last item refers, I believe, to the whole picture that Pascal draws of man-without-God, which depends on proofs drawn from nature. Items 1, 2, 9, and 10 are just on the verge of turning into explicit proofs of the kind I have discussed above in detail. They suggest the paradoxes (nos. 1 and 2) and the convincing qualities (nos. 9 and 10) that might easily lead to explicit propositions and proofs.

Moreover, the list in fragment 482 contains previous clues to Pascal's view of how a religious conversion might take place.

> Il est indubitable qu'après cela on ne doit pas refuser, en considérant ce que c'est que la vie, et que cette religion, de suivre l'inclination de la suivre, si elle nous vient dans le coeur; et il est certain qu'il n'y a nul lieu de se moquer de ceux qui la suivent.

"Après cela": that backward glance invites the mind to sum up all the proofs bearing on this life and this religion (nature and Scripture once more) that have been adduced, and to recognize that its natural desire for truth and under-standing have been met. Indifference, hostility, skep-ticism—insofar as they depend on views subject to reasoning—must give way, Pascal thinks. The obstacles are lifted, the way is cleared, and the next decisive event may occur. The heart may find itself inclined to assent, and if that happens, there will be no ground for objection on the side of intellect, and no reason not to follow that inspi-ration. Both mind and heart are involved in belief. The Apologist marshals the arguments for the first; the rest comes from God. Only one thing is missing, the "Machine" (and it is implied, in part), the force of habit, that comes from acting repeatedly as though one believed. For the complete account we may turn again to fragment 808 (fragment 418, the *pari*, would do almost as well, though it is much longer). In those six lines Pascal explains himself with great clarity and concision:

Il y a trois moyens de croire: la raison, la coutume, l'inspiration. La religion chrétienne qui seule a la raison n'admet point pour ses vrais enfants ceux qui croient sans inspiration. Ce n'est pas qu'elle exclue la raison et la coutume, au contraire; mais il faut ouvrir son esprit aux preuves, s'y confirmer par la coutume, mais s'offrir par les humiliations aux inspirations, qui seules peuvent faire le vrai et salutaire effet, *ne evacuetur crux Christi*.

The last of the means is crucial, for without it there can be no genuine Christian faith, but that faith does not exclude the other two. Far from it: proofs enlighten the mind; custom strengthens them by adding to the firmness with which one holds them; inspiration works then the true salutary effect in the heart.

Proofs, the Pensées and Beyond

A study of proofs in the *Pensées* is rewarding and valuable for several reasons. (1) It helps us to make sense out of the phenomenal surface of the work, to grasp its features as deriving from a tissue of proofs, in spite of the fact that many premises are shortened or implied, and to direct ourselves along the paths that lead in Pascal's view to rational certainty. He recognizes the value of geometry as a model, but does not in fact incorporate geometrical reasoning into more than a sprinkling of fragments. He recognizes, also, the relevance of deistic metaphysics as a possible source of proofs, as a science in which questions of interest to him have been raised and answered; but, again, he sets this kind of thinking aside as being too complicated and too technical. Instead he chooses reasoning that is close to common sense and experience. We are prompted by his practice to distinguish four tendencies of proof that appear in acts of composition, definition, reconciliation, and intervention. And we should not overlook the fact that the

absence of proof may be an argument in favor of proposition.
(2) It helps us to see, as we read the *Pensées*, the contexts
(the principal ones being Nature and Scripture) that mark
off stages in reasoning and in the determination of meaning. Since proofs occur apropos of topics which derive
from contexts, to study them is one way of disengaging
and identifying the contexts. It is only in the light of such
local frameworks that we can effectively recover two essential things: the particular affinities and counterrelation-
ships that Pascal's terms and words have toward one
another, and the specific realities to which his vocabulary
refers. His personal habit of language, with some of its
peculiarities of connotation and denotation, becomes accessible, and we can glimpse through that the underlying
mental states and tensions that give rise to the text. (3) The
study of proof and proofs also makes it easier than it
otherwise would be to locate the ultimate principles on
which the projected Apology and the *Pensées* (as distinct
from and including the Apology) are based. We soon become aware of what is surely one of the main themes—if
not the main theme—in Pascal's thought, the quest for
certainty, and of the two centers of initiative in which certainty originates, man and God. Man, Pascal, the
Apologist can furnish the rational preparation, in itself a
subsidiary kind of certainty, for the final kind, which is a
God-given inclination that cannot deceive. We begin to see
the bearing of these principles on the question of bringing
the nonbeliever into the company of believers and the
question of justifying the special place of Christianity vis-
à-vis other religions. No apologist can avoid these two
problems, and Pascal's proofs, according to one possible
division, are adapted by turns to one or the other. (4)
Moreover, by studying proofs we can clarify the implications of two phrases that regulate almost everything in the
Pensées: "croire sans preuves" and "croire avec preuves."
The former, the way of unmediated inclination alone, is

always sufficient; the latter, the way of the seeker Pascal has in mind for his Apology (and, no doubt, the way of Pascal himself), includes an element of reasoning that is necessary but never sufficient. To understand this is to understand why Pascal, after the immense effort spent on showing the role of reason as a finder of proofs, still insists on the place of the Machine and of inspiration. (5) Finally, a study of Pascal's tendencies regarding proofs, and specifically, of the four lines along which they appear to run, sheds light on his practice in his other works, especially the scientific treatises, where the logical themes are introduced and combined differently, and it provides a starting point for further investigation of any theme in particular. In the *Pensées*, for example, one thing is clear: the hints of geometry that we have found are far from being the only traces of science in the "thoughts on religion and some other subjects."

Nearer at hand is a subject that can be worked out in the fragments themselves. Pascal surely thought of the proofs as elements destined to be disposed in a certain order. As he writes at the end of fragment 427:

> Mais pour ceux qui y apporteront une sincérité parfaite et un véritable désir de rencontrer la vérité, j'espère qu'ils auront satisfaction, et qu'ils seront convaincus des preuves d'une religion si divine, que j'ai ramassées ici, et dans lesquelles j'ai suivi à peu près cet ordre...

An inquiry into proofs brings us inevitably to the need for an understanding of *ordre*.

2 | Order and Orders

Three
Senses | The word "ordre" appears so frequently in the *Pensées*—it even serves as the title of the first *liasse* of the papers assembled by Pascal for his Apology—that there can be no doubt of its importance when one attempts to recover the meaning of the *Pensées* and to see what the underlying assumptions are. But the word becomes really interesting when we look at it as a term, as a word with a meaning (or meanings) fixed by the author for his particular purpose. In the case of *ordre*, the word actually stands for more than one term and has more than one meaning. I think three lines of thought and association may be detected: (1) order as a sequence or arrangement; (2) order as an area or domain, as setting the boundaries within which all members of a certain category situate themselves; and, finally, (3) order as an imperative, as a command given by someone of authority.

Examples of the three senses may be found early in the *Pensées*.

+ Ordre par dialogues.
Que dois-je faire. Je ne vois partout qu'obscurités.
Croirai-je que je ne suis rien? Croirai-je que je suis dieu?

These lines form the whole of fragment 2. They pose the first sense, that of sequence, and include both a suggestion of the elements to be ordered (dialogues) and a promising starting point for one of those elements. The other two senses of "command" and "domain" appear in fragment 14:

> Les vrais chrétiens obéissent aux folies néanmoins, non pas qu'ils respectent les folies, mais l'*ordre de Dieu* qui pour la punition des hommes les a affermis à ces folies.... Ainsi saint Thomas explique le lieu de saint Jacques pour la préférence des riches, que s'ils ne le font dans la vue de Dieu ils sortent de l'*ordre de la religion*. (Italics added.)

For our present purpose, which concerns the structure and movement of Pascalian discourse, senses (1) and (2) are particularly relevant. Without neglecting entirely the third sense, let us here concentrate on the others. I have found twenty instances where "ordre" means sequence or arrangement, and in them there is a clearly discernible pattern. As we study it, though, we should always remember that we are dealing with an unfinished work, the parts or remains of which show distinct signs of varying degrees of finish. Even when the evidence is compelling, our conclusions must be tentative, for the texts themselves are tentative and partial elaborations of what Pascal had in mind. (Where the *niveau de rédaction* speaks for a finished or nearly finished version, one that has been carefully worked over, it is still preferable to make this assumption.) A thought in movement and still seeking its definitive expression: that is what we must try to recover and reflect in our analyses. Moreover, although the Apology and its requirements must have a special claim to our attention, they do not regulate everything, for many fragments do not immediately pertain to the persuasion and conversion of *libertins* but contain instead ideas intended for other uses, at times only distantly related to the apologetic end.

Elements and Structures

In the first group of texts one must distinguish, it would seem, between two aspects in any order. There is the sequence or arrangement itself, and there is the collection of elements that enter into the order. On this point, as on many points in the *Pensées,* the reader is soon aware, as he compares the fragments, of different degrees of explicitness. Sometimes Pascal only hints at one or the other of the aspects. Sometimes he gives such clear indications that we know precisely what is being ordered and how.

Another striking thing is the diversity in the elements: They give us readily a great deal of evidence regarding the range of data in Pascal's mind as he ponders or uses the idea of order. He sees events and actions as in fragment 329 (on predictions) or in 451 (on the history of the Jews); the members of the body or its faculties, as in 421 (on the subordination of the parts of the body, including the power of willing, to the good of the whole body), and to this might be added 106, where he sees men drawing out of the operation of concupiscence "un si bel ordre" in society: he is probably thinking of classes, customs, laws, *métiers,* which may have an irrational and even vicious source but still allow men to live together in relative peace and partial justice. Or, again, and here we find the richest vein, he sees elements of discourse and thought. He applies the idea of order to a list that runs the entire range from the smallest to the largest unit: words, thoughts, truths, distinctions, topics ("matières"), principles, proofs, dialogues, letters, discourses.[1] He moves back and forth between external expressions and forms on the one hand,

and inner forms—progressions, developments, outlines
—on the other. In the former group, he mentions
large expository units such as the letter and the dialogue;
in the latter he refers to the *parties*, *matières*, principles,
truths, thoughts that are to appear eventually as the contents of those expository units.

Some elements—letters and dialogues, for example—
take on the dimensions of ordering structures and lead us
to the idea of order in itself. We know already the species:
organic, as in bodies; historical, as in accounts of events;
discursive, as in most of the instances where "ordre" occurs, and indeed, in the *Pensées* as in some sense a single
work of apology and of meditation on selcted themes.
Along with the idea of order in and by itself one of the
most fundamental things in the thought of Pascal makes its
appearance: his conception of certainty—that necessary
concomitant of truth—and of the ways that open access to
it. One means of reaching it is through demonstrations that
move from antecedents to consequents and through sequences of such demonstrations. Geometry sets the ideal,
for that science approximates discursive order in its pure
state. In opposition to it is another approach to truth that is
immediate and intuitive. The workings of sense provide
the model. I am aware of Pascal's distrust of the senses, but
those *puissances trompeuses* are not always wrong, and the
self-evidence of sensation prefigures a decisive experience
that is not in fact linked to any of the five senses. The heart
knows the first principles of science (space, movement,
time, number) in a way—by *sentiment*—that is not and
cannot be demonstrated; after those intuitions occur, reason has something to work with in its task of mediation
and discourse on the way to warranted conclusions. Much
of what Pascal says about *ordre* stems clearly from this conception of reasoning, which is linear, propositional,
theorematic, and based on undeniable insights. (We know

that he did not believe intuition to be rational; in this he differs from Descartes.)

And just as clearly, it seems to me, when he finds himself obliged to recognize other orders that lead to certainty, he tends to conceive them as deviations or removes from geometry and its procedures. He does what we all do, which is to try to grasp the less well-known via what is better-known to us. After telling us in fragment 694 that in order to show the vanity of ordinary lives (*vies communes*), and then the vanity of philosopher's lives by the examples of the Stoics and Pyrrhonians, he adds:

> . . .mais l'ordre ne serait pas gardé. Je sais un peu ce que c'est, et combien peu de gens l'entendent. Nulle science humaine ne le peut garder. Saint Thomas ne l'a pas gardé. La mathématique le garde, mais elle est inutile en sa profondeur.

What does Pascal substitute for the order of mathematics? He moves, in the first place, toward an enveloping order that is a mixture of dialectic and rhetoric. Dialectic supplies a way of posing problems, a technique that turns on the statement of contradictions and on the search for the means of resolving them. Rhetoric prolongs the dialectic, addressing itself to the needs of the reader and inventing the means that will cause desired changes in his ideas and attitudes. That describes succinctly, I think, what Pascal does, in fact, as he leaves behind the formalities of geometry, which no human science, no science of man, can observe. Actually he does not stop at the foregoing stage, which has provided a rough scenario: the study of the vanity and wretchedness of man through the *contrariétés*, the recognition of the need for something like a faith-seeking posture, and then the appeals to the Bible. At each of these or similar steps he has the option of using another order—that of Jesus Christ, Saint Paul, and Saint

Augustine, who seek not to instruct but to excite ("échauffer"), warm, or inflame.

> Cet ordre consiste principalement à la digression sur chaque point qui a rapport à la fin, pour la montrer toujours. (Fr. 298)

Thus, in addition to the linear progressions of mathematical order and the more flexible sequences of dialectic and rhetoric, Pascal defines a local order that is at once digressive and convergent. Its episodes leave the basic line of reasoning and yet are never really apart from it, because the intended end is always in sight. The presence of the end in that kind of discourse makes it possible for us to understand another passage on order and to isolate still another principle of composition.

> J'écrirai ici mes pensées sans ordre et non pas peut-être dans une confusion sans dessein. C'est le véritable ordre et qui marquera toujours mon objet par le désordre même.
>
> Je ferais trop d'honneur à mon sujet si je le traitais avec ordre puisque je veux montrer qu'il en est incapable. (Fr. 532)

At the head of this entry Pascal wrote "Pyrr." This is the order of the Pyrrhonian thinker. A disorder that is still an order and, indeed, the true and authentic order: the paradox is typical of Pascal's way with words and meanings. If the preceding nongeometric methods are progressive and digressive, may we not call this one expressive? It tells us something about the skeptic and his thought over and above what the words may signify directly. A curious inversion or reversion has taken place. The order of Christ, Saint Paul, and Saint Augustine, though digressive, looks forward *toujours* to the end; the Pyrrhonian order looks backward *toujours* to the subject being treated and expresses that subject's nature.

Powers, Operations, Objects

The term "order" has, then, three basic meanings for Pascal in the *Pensées*: sequence or arrangement, category of beings, command. The first of these meanings appears in at least three distinct contexts—that of historical events, that of bodies composed of interrelated members, and that of demonstration and persuasion. Further examination of this last context has shown something like a scale of ordering activiites, from (1) the definitions, axioms, and tight sequences of geometry to (2) the progressive but not strictly linear movement of dialectic through stages determined by the inner logic of Pascal's position and by his conception of the conversion-experience that he is fostering in his reader to (3) something less formal, less comprehensive, more episodic and self-contained (although a unifying principle is always in the back of his mind) to (4) something even more relaxed and disorganized, an uninhibited transcription of one's ideas, one after another as they come (although here, too, the disorder hides a special kind of intelligibility). And all of these arrangements, which are basically discursive and linked to temporal succession, take their place opposite intuitive thought that grasps a multiplicity in a different way, by a unifying act of vision in which all relevant parts or elements are present simultaneously.[2]

Three kinds of order—progressive, digressive, expressive—are surely to tbe found in the *Pensées*. We may safely say, however, that Pascal's projects there lead him to favor the first and second types (nos. 2 and 3 above). They require discipline rather than unreflective spontaneity. To understand these more rigorous kinds of order, we need to consider briefly what lies before them in faculties and operations and what follows from them in logical style and structure.

One may discern in certain fragments a traditional set of

psychological notions, though Pascal does not draw attention to them explicitly. Why should he bother, since a particular specification of them is what counts for him? But it
is enlightening for us to recognize their presence. The
terms are scholastic in origin: power/habit/operation/object.
All of these factors may be found at work in fragments 511,
512, 513, and 751, where Pascal makes distinctions among
the various types of minds ("esprits"). There is less about
habit than about the other three terms, but it is not neglected entirely. As for the powers, they finally are reduced
to two insofar as knowing and ordering are concerned:
esprit and *cœur*. It is true that in fragment 511 Pascal
analyzes, compares, and contrasts what he calls the "esprit
de géométrie" and the "esprit de finesse." But he uses
words there in a way that obliges us, I think, to connect
the *esprit de finesse* with *cœur* if we consider at the same time
fragment 512 along with fragments 511, 513, 751, and 298.
The scheme that emerges involves two opposed powers
correlated with two pairs of operations focusing on different
objects. To be specific, we may say that both mind and heart
work by intuition and by movement based on intuition. But
the characteristic operations for the mind are *voir* and *raison-
ner*, with emphasis on the latter (though it would be absurd
to neglect the intuitive moment because the truth of consequences depends on the correctness of an original act of
seeing). The characteristic operations of the heart, though
analogous to those of the mind, call for different words,
"sentir" and "juger" (Pascal is not always consistent, but
the tendency is unmistakable), so that the emphasis falls
on intuitive and nearly-intuitive thinking or knowing (but
it would be wrong to leave out all reference to discursive
motions).

Now the objects on which these powers and operations
are exercised are *principes,* which differ in number and in
kind. The *esprit de géométrie* works on a relatively small
number, while the *esprit de finesse* must deal with a great

number, a number so great that a principle may easily be
omitted or overlooked. And this first distinguishing characteristic is linked to another that is more a matter of kind.
The geometrical mind turns away from commonly experienced reality to principles that are, in Pascal's words, "hors
d'usage," whereas the *esprit de finesse,* in its specific operations, deals with factors and principles that are before
everyone's eyes, even though he describes them at one
point in fragment 512 as being hard to see (possibly because they are so numerous). The former type may be isolated and handled ("maniés"), and they are communi-
cable; but one has great difficulty in causing others to feel
("faire sentir aux autres") the principles on which the *esprit
de finesse* bases itself. The products of these diverse powers
and principles are reasonings or demonstrations as opposed to sentiments or judgments, and they embody different orders, one being elaborate, full, continuous, while
the other is untechnical, digressive, and relatively discon-
tinuous.

Assent and Argument

All sequences follow, therefore, from ordering powers,
their lines of operation, and their objects. Seen in this way,
they tend to fall into extremes of (1) reasoning demonstratively or (2) judging intuitively, even spontaneously.[3]
The truth of the matter would seem to be that on occasion
Pascal feels the need to distinguish them thus clearly, but
more often steers a course somewhere between the two. In
the apologetic portion of the *Pensées* he seeks to be logical
without being technical and deductive; he wants to be ap-
pealing, but he must be more than purely intuitive. This
movement away from the extremes of geometry and
finesse—however useful the distinctions may have been for
clarity of analysis—yields a progressive method that
blends rhetoric and dialectic. In its first or interpersonal

aspect, we have a clearly indicated line that moves through a succession of points set by the itinerary of the reader or interlocutor as he assents and as his attitude evolves. In its second aspect the method is dialectical and logical, for the critical changes in the seeker correspond to the critical points in the argument being advanced by the Apologist. These parallel lines furnish the plot of a moral drama and its logical correlate, and the two factors determine each other: *causae ad invicem* . . . .[4]

The Moral Drama

The projected sequence of the Apology, insofar as the large blocks of apologetic substance are concerned, derives in fact from the reader, from the person to be persuaded rather than from the argument purely and simply.[5] The mechanism of assent and the stages implied by it set the moral plot. There is a beginning, middle, and end, each corresponding to a mental and moral state: indifference, search, and active waiting for divine inspiration.

The first two make up the field of action for Pascal; there he can deploy all his talents as thinker and rhetorician. By intellectual and moral shocks, warmed by irony, sarcasm, indignation, or charity, he intends to bring the unbeliever to the point of accepting the proposition that one must search. That will serve as a pivot for transition to the second main phase, which has to be somewhat more complicated, since Pascal writes to "faire croire nos deux pièces," the mind and the heart—and in that order. We have a reprise of the shock technique, but Pascal uses it much more methodically, having gained the attention of his reader-listener. Again and again, indefatigably, he points out how much justice, truth, and happiness man wants and how little of those he has and can have. Then he turns the shambles of our hopes into a dazzling paradox: along with all this wretchedness there remains an inextinguishable greatness, even though it takes the form of pride most often. And the paradox moves: one does not simply look at it and react to it; one is called upon to undergo the *renversement continuel du pour au contre*, as Pascal shifts his direction, pulling us upward and downward by turns.

At the end of this process, in the fact of our incomprehensibility—for we are in the midst of a discussion of reason and what it can understand of our condition—we look for some principle of explanation. Pascal tells us that it is the mystery of original sin. That represents one degree of intelligibility, one step in the pacifying of the mind and the removal of its obstacles. That retrospective view toward Eden and its loss is balanced by the discussion of whether we can know the existence and nature of God, which turns into the *pari*. Pascal cannot be more positive here because of the disproportion between finite knowers and the infinite Being to be known. His conclusion, essentially prospective, to the effect that belief in God is not contrary to reason, gives the mind a defensible position that is not hostile to religion (indifference was left behind much earlier).[6] Christianity has understood man and his contradictory nature—and so can we in the light of its doctrine; then calculation of our interest in the future completes the arguments addressed to the mind.

"But I cannot believe," says the second speaker at the end of the wager, and Pascal shifts his attention to the passions, those emotional principles that attach us to the things of this world. His formula is simple. One forms the new disposition by doing, by repeatedly *acting as if* the Christian religion were true. And so, after harmonizing by a probability faith with reason, after causing the reader to hope that the content of that faith is true, Pascal leaves him with a new way of behaving (that has God as its provisional end) and a new way of thinking (that concentrates on proofs from Scripture, so that the underside of the game may become apparent), both of which are essentially receptive and open to the initiative of God. The whole sense of the apologetic part of the *Pensées* consists in this: that it is possible for a man to prepare in himself the *viam Domini,* by listening to someone who can satisfy at least partially his mind and by acting on advice as to the means of moderating his passions.

The Ideological Parallel

That open-ended psychological and moral drama, thus divided into three acts, unifies or would have unified the presentation that Pascal seems to have intended. But there is another *ordre,* intimately associated with the personal evolution just sketched: an order that is ideological rather than psychological and moral. Words and terms evolve also; the action of the argument parallels the action of the drama. In this second and matching sequence, we can observe the traits and consequences of dialectical reasoning. The discourse is interpersonal (at least partly); it clarifies words, thoughts, and things simultaneously; it does not separate outer (real) from inner (mental) processes and thus lead to technical or scientific investigation; it starts with, works with, and ends with common experience and what we can make of it under Pascal's guiding hand.

The whole undertaking hinges on the antithesis, *l'homme sans Dieu* and *l'homme avec Dieu.* Thus every important subject treated falls into the negative phase of the argument for a while, before passing into the positive phase; every salient word or term takes on a different value, according to the regime under which it appears. In the first perspective Pascal multiplies contradictions, *contrariétés,* and frustrations; paradoxes abound, and the possibility of certainty fades into perplexity and doubt. In the second perspective a unifying principle emerges (actually, its hidden presence leads to the confusion noted in the first part of the argument: I mean, the fact that it is hidden makes that confusion inevitable), and it becomes possible to resolve the

various pulls and tensions into unity when one relates
everything to that absolute principle. What seemed to be a
discussion heading for skepticism turns into something as-
sertive and sure of itself.[7] The main subject of inquiry (man)
ceases to be contradictory, full of conflicting ties to the
world, a battleground where struggle is renewed over and
over again, and becomes instead a double thirst that is
actually one thirst, one tendency toward faith and
beatitude. Against this background of recurrent devices
that are certainly not the invention of Pascal—he simply
rediscovered their long-standing possibilities—the ideological plot, the ballet of terms, takes its specific form.

In the first part of the *recherche,* for example, with the
ideas of infinite Justice and Truth and Good in the back of
his mind, Pascal has no difficulty in exposing the shams,
egoisms, inadequacies, and shortcomings that surround
us. He draws a violent contrast between what man wants
or thinks he has and what his lot actually is in society, in
moral relationships, and in knowledge. Pascal applies his
absolute criterion—apparently threefold, consisting of
Truth, Justice, and Good, but actually one and the same—
to the state of man as acting by nature, without the benefit
of any gifts or strengths coming from beyond nature. He
therefore emphasizes the distance between the criterion
and what he judges. In the second phase of his argument,
he must readjust all the important terms of his analysis.
The essential thing is this: the judged, no longer opposed
to the criterion, begins to organize itself and to orient itself
toward the criterion as end. Man and nature (especially
human nature) become theotropic. What had been a principle of judgment and the cause of despair, a means of
obtaining insight into incomprehensible *contrariétés,* turns
into a principle of love, mercy, hope, reconciliation.

At the same time, Pascal is able to identify the principles
that spoil nature: original sin, and what is even more fundamental, self-love, which caused original sin. Triumphant before the change in the attitude of the *chercheur* (as

he has become) and before the change in the dialectical framework, self-love must now give way and by a radical purification become the love of God. What was a scene of disorder among things, people, and powers of heart and mind turns into a situation where things, people, and powers fit ideally into a hierarchy. After the oscillation between *ennui* and distraction, ignorance and dogmatism, misery and pride—an essentially repetitive cycle—comes progress in time and place toward realizing the hierarchy. (Before the shift to the positive side of the dialectic, being, time, place, and the existential questions to which they give rise—why *am* I, *here* and *now?*—had no answers.)

In the first part of the argument we are obliged to recognize in Nature the presence of problems that appear insoluble. Even when we move into the second phase, centered on Scripture, contradiction presides over the discussion—until the semantic device of figurative interpretation has done its work, and unified the record given in the Old and New Testaments. Then that single story may be brought to bear on the problems of Nature hitherto *sibi relicta;* and it brings Nature into line with the ideal ends of truth, justice, and happiness, which subsist as one in God. Pascal intends, of course, to present a cumulative view of Nature at first by itself, then subsumed under Scripture (though not dismissed by it), Nature judged and then redeemed. My point is that he meshes these changes of semantic and logical perspective with the changes of attitude and conviction going on in his reader. Indifference, transition, search, transition, humble readiness: these stages and the stages of the argument imply and reinforce each other; rhetoric and dialectic concur.

Recapitulation

In the foregoing paragraphs we have seen what order as sequence means in the *Pensées,* and we have analyzed in detail the working of that term in the context of an Apology. Although Pascal's idea of sequence may be and is applied to many different things, what seems particularly valuable in interpreting the fragments is its use as a principle of exposition. He actually defines three possibilities: the order of the Pyrrhonian, a random sequence based on association of ideas and pure self-expression; the order of the heart, which is spontaneous and digressive, but unified by a supreme principle; and the order of the mind, which he tends to equate with the impersonal chain-reasoning found in geometry. These three correspond to the presence or absence of control and to the dominance of this or that faculty. None of these is, I think, entirely satisfactory for understanding the apologetic portions of the *Pensées,* nor is a simple combination of them specific enough. They do, however, help us to define his way of proceeding.

He certainly does not choose the order of chance, nor the impersonal demonstrations of geometry, the first being too self-centered, too disorderly, and the second too technical and laborious. In my opinion he adopts the order of the heart, but he adds a new dimension by intellectualizing it. He wants to be sensitive to the feelings of his reader, but he wants also to have the advantages of sequence in carefully reasoned discourse. No method that failed to make connection with the mind and heart of the person addressed could possibly satisfy him. In dialectic, as disciplined interpersonal thinking designed to bring about agreement, he appears to have found the perfect answer. (That Pascal never gives the name of dialectic to his method is beside the point.) On the logical side it progresses by means of radical shifts in the context of the argument, and by the antitheses and resolutions made possible in this way. It has the movement and order that Pascal liked; it has also great adaptability to changes in topics and occasions, since it may at any time appeal to a readily available overriding end, which imparts relevance to any episode, and, through the force of analogy, makes it pertinent to all other sections of the work. This logic of conflict and reconciliation may be adjusted nicely to a rhetoric that is an art of puzzlement and ultimate insight and conversion.

Thus dialectic, with its peculiar logical and persuasive capabilities, solves the problem of apologetic method for Pascal. Of course there are various species of dialectic: I do not mean to use the term as though it could be defined unambiguously even in the *Pensées*. The fragments show traces—indeed, more than that: the characteristic lines—of a skeptical, suspensive dialectic, which is associated with Montaigne, Epicureans, and Pyrrhonians, and of a reductive dialectic which is attached to the Stoics and their ideal of bringing human and providential wills into conformity. But the species that prevails in the fragments does not end in mutually refuting opinions proposed by men or in the harmony of wills arising from and returning to Nature; it brings its multiplicities to final unity in a single supernatural perspective.[8] In Hegel and Marx the bases are metaphysical and historical rather than interpersonal. Hegelian dialectic moves toward the Absolute Idea, and Marxist dialectic toward the classless society, while the interpersonal dialectic of Pascal strives for unanimity and, after that, for beatitude.

Order as Domain: Separation and Proportion

The study of Pascal's usage takes us eventually to the second main meaning of *ordre:* from order as sequence, and especially as expository sequence, to order as category, level of being, problem area, meeting place of opposed ideas and people. Order in this new sense appears frequently in the plural, which is consistent with the fact that Pascal usually has recourse to it when he is expounding a hierarchy. It leads in a vertical direction, away from the horizontal distinctions and linear movements that have characterized his logic and rhetoric so far. In short, it leads into his metaphysics and theology.

Pascal makes his principles explicit in fragment 308, but the less elaborate treatment in fragment 933, with its slight variations in diction and less exalted tone, gives valuable clues to the network of verbal associations from which he works. In both fragment 308 and fragment 933 he lists three orders, but on occasion he may give only partial views of the total scheme because of changes in the context and circumstances of the argument. His impulse in the fuller account (fr. 308) is to separate and to put as much distance as possible between the three realms of *corps, esprits,* and *charité.* The break is radical between the first two; it pales, though, in comparison with the abyss between the second and third terms. When we have grasped something of the infinite distance that separates the two substances of body and mind, we must try, mustering all our powers of insight, to grasp a distinction that is infinitely more distinguishing than the preceding one. And yet, it is a curious thing, Pascal invites us to see these orders as entering into a system, a set of proportions. He uses essentially the same language apropos of all three; he relies on the power of analogy in words and ideas to keep the elements of his vision from flying apart; and since analogy implies difference as well as likeness, he can pull things together and at the same time emphasize in the strongest way their disparity. The tension he develops between these two inherent directions of analogical thinking is enormous.

Let us look for a moment at what is proper to each of these realms. On the level of bodies, flesh, and sense, one meets the princes, the powerful, the captains, the wealthy: they have their activities and exertions, their battles and victories. On the level of minds, one meets the great representatives of the intellect: they, too, have problems to

solve, discoveries to make, and inventions to work out—
Archimedes is the exemplary figure. On the level of charity, love, and the heart, one meets the saints, and Jesus
Christ is the great exemplar: his life, death, resurrection,
and victory give supreme expression to the realities and
trials of this domain. Each plane has its people, its obstacles and contradictions, its successes and its glories. The
great figures, Pascal says, all have characteristic luster and
brilliance, to a degree from the outset, but decidedly after
their victories. Fragment 933 adds a few details to this picture. The saints correspond to the wise ("sages") in the
new formulation, the representatives of the mind are described as "curieux," as "savants"; the realm of charity
("charité") in fragment 308 is analogous to that of will
("volonté") in 933; and the end ("objet") on each level is
defined as body, mind, and justice or righteousness.

An essential device of the dialectical method makes its
appearance in fragment 933 when Pascal writes, "Dieu doit
régner sur tout et tout se rapporter à lui." It was present in
308, but only by implication. It is the comprehensive final
principle needed to maintain the hierarchy of the orders.
And Pascal says more clearly in fragment 933 than in 308
what happens when this principle is absent or neglected:
the onset of *concupiscence de la chair, concupiscence des yeux,*
and *orgueil.* In other words, by introducing the trio of concupiscence, curiosity, and pride, he adds the possibility of
specifically improper motivation on each level. In fragment
308, Pascal underlines the distinction and the isolation of
the orders; in 933 he relates them to their final end—as
opposed to the ends proper to each of them—and suggests
that a negative counterpart shadows the activities of each
plane, vitiating them whenever one loses sight of that last
object, that final Person.

Since people are active on all three levels, one may won-
der whether everyone can see and interpret what is going
on. The answer is obviously *no* for Pascal, and that fact
points up something inherent in his pattern of thought

here. Let us phrase the question in more general terms. Taking the orders and their realities and actions as objects of knowledge, what powers of knowing do they imply?[9] From the fragments in which Pascal evokes the majesty of nature or the infinite character of God, we have learned that in order to know, there must be a proportion between the knower and the known (actually, those fragments have proved to us the *dis*proportion between man and what he would like to grasp with his powers). Pascal connects explicitly two of the orders with knowing powers, *esprit* and *cœur;* indeed they give their names to their respective orders. he does not say so outright, but he associates sense with *corps,* and by an odd twist makes this implied power of knowing into the source of his vocabulary for discussing the other two. He speaks of what is "visible" or "invisible" on the level of *esprit,* and of "les yeux du coeur." The obvious advantages and successes of those on the lowest level have no luster for people whose lives center on matters of the mind. Pascal does not go so far as to say that the great intellects cannot see what lies on the level of body and flesh, but he says without hesitation that the fleshly ones, the "charnels," cannot discern the greatness of those above, whose domain, victories, and glories (though very real) are visible not to eyes but to minds. Looking from above once more, Pascal assures us likewise that the greatness of wisdom and the magnificence of Jesus Christ, both on the top level and known through the eyes of the heart, are invisible to those whose usual sphere of activity is the mind as well as to those who live in the flesh. The world of mind is closed to sense, and the world of holiness or of the heart is closed to mind (and all the more so to sense).

Of course, the realities in each order may be objects of desire as well as of knowing. The repeated references in fragment 933 to concupiscence leave no doubt of that. Pascal's way of expressing himself sometimes seems contradictory, as he does not abide by literal restrictions of terms to particular levels, but he lets us see the outline of a coherent picture. If we are to discuss concupiscence, we begin with the heart, the center of affectivity, of desire and aversion, and then proceed to distinguish between negative and morally wanting impulses on the one hand, and on the other, positive, morally justified wishes. The former he calls "concupiscence"; the latter, the correct form of desire, because it seeks God first of all with penitence and humility, is "charité." A slight problem arises when this distinction is applied to the three orders. It seems that concupiscence may do its work on every level, and so the heart is involved everywhere: one finds expressions like "concupiscence de la chair" and "concupiscence des yeux" (the context shows that this applies to the level of mind) in fragment 933. But the specific form taken by concupiscence when one seeks things of the flesh is also "concupiscence"! On the level above, its typical form is "curiosité," and on the top level, "orgueil." Pascal uses the term now in a broad sense, now in a narrow sense. He generally limits the positive inclinations of the heart to the top level of holiness and charity. If there is a suggestion of values to be desired and sought on the lower levels, it falls no doubt under his principle, "Dieu doit régner sur tout et tout se rapporter à lui." The natural tendency of his thought is to see the negative things on the lower rungs of his ladder and to slip into positive associations at the top. In this he follows the movements generally characteristic of Augustinianism, which is haunted by ultimate values and inclined to minimize if not overlook those which are intermediate or remote.

Interrelations of Levels

Battles and victories, inventions and productions, inclinations and insights, kinds of brilliance and greatness all vary according to the order, each being knowable to or accessible to a particular human faculty. The infinite distances between the orders lead Pascal to assure us in the strongest language that we shall never get thought out of bodies, no matter how impressive they may seem in the sky or in all the kingdoms of the earth. Nor shall we ever be able to extract the tiniest charitable impulse ("mouvement de cha- rité") from the mind and its productions, to say nothing of the impossibility of doing so from corporeal things. But as we know from his view of man, Pascal likes *renversements,* and I think much of the most interesting substance of the *Pensées*—in their apologetic function—comes from the in- terrelations and interactions of the orders. When intellec- tual problems must be solved, sparks that bridge the gaps between the orders make explanations possible. The fact is that Pascal, in spite of his diverse tendencies in method and proof, usually returns to one—the dialectical—and, consequently, he looks for the truth *in system.* This means that he arrives at moments when he must arrange the dif- ferent levels according to a recurrent scale that depends on an ultimate principle. It also means that he cannot isolate completely any problem on any level. What happens in a lower order cannot be satisfactorily explained unless all that lies above it is taken into account. What he finds on any lower level, as he views it from above, is opposition and paradox, tension and rivalry, contradiction and inter- mittence. Always eager to locate the *raison des effets* or to apply some *idée de derrière,* Pascal then moves the opposi- tions toward harmony and repose, either temporary or lasting.

His way of working along the line of scientific and geometrical knowing gives us a striking example. To understand it we must recall the two moments involved in knowing (they may even be thought of as two kinds of knowing): the intuitive and the discursive. Before the latter can begin we must have bases that only the former can provide. At the beginning of fragment 418 Pascal tells us, in a violent image, not unexpected in view of the extreme form his dualism takes, that the soul is cast into the body—"jetée dans le corps"—and then that it finds in bodies "nombre," "temps," "dimensions," on which it may begin its work of reasoning. These ideas are the means by which it takes hold of bodies in order to determine their natures and to focus on the necessities that regulate their activities.[10] Here the order of *esprits* is coming into contact with the order of *corps;* somehow the radical separation so noticeable in fragment 308 is abated. But where does reason get those ideas? Fragment 418 simply says that it finds them in bodies; they may be applied in discourse about bodies. For the origins of these instruments of knowing, we may go to fragment 110, where Pascal is defending some certainties from the Pyrrhonians, as they mount their fierce attack on the dogmatists. "Nous connaissons la vérité non seulement par la raison mais encore par le cœur." We know that life is not a dream; we know the difference between being asleep and being awake. Other certainties known by the heart and by instinct include first principles such as space, time, motion, and number. The third order has provided the second order with the means, the conceptual tools it needs, for interpreting the opacities and multiplicities found on the first order. Distinctions of levels but cooperation among them that respects their different ranks: such is the formula.

Along the lines and byways of moral thought, as Pascal offers his analysis of human affairs, we can make out the same pattern in a form equally striking though somewhat less obvious. When he begins to survey with his interlocutor-reader the spectacle of human action—individual and social—he evokes a scene full of agitation, of turnings to every side in search of diversion; or if not that, a scene of action according to customs that are variable and capricious. But the whole show begins to make a somber kind of sense when he brings on as criteria the

ideas of truth and justice. Seen from above, the order of
the *charnels*, the wealthy, the kings, the princes—and that
of the *peuple* as well—becomes intelligible: "la nature est
corrompue." All that movement, all that illusion-filled
busyness comes into a kind of focus when from the level of
reflective mind we make our judgments in the light of the
twin ideals—truth and justice—inherent in our nature.
They not only pose the ends of action but also state the
principles of moral understanding. At the next step, which
occurs primarily on the level of mind and thought, an antithesis appears, the wretchedness and greatness of man;
and we shall be doomed to shuttle endlessly between those
poles, unless we reach upward from the planes of nature
and intellect and take the key to the riddle from the plane
of supernature, heart, and faith. That key is, of course, the
idea of a mysterious original sin and of its equally mysterious transmission. The contradictions of the *charnels* become explicable as deficiencies when referred to moral
principles; and the deficiencies, when visualized more
fully on the level of thought tend to become a single, great,
and enigmatic contradiction; and that, in its turn, becomes
a two-sided truth in the obscure light of religious doctrine.
Can one not glimpse a further movement upward? The
heart, too, knows changes and oscillations. As a necessary
continuation of Pascal's thought, may we not say that beyond existence in a world where it knows it cannot be
finally at ease, the heart looks forward to beatitude and the
end of mobility and conflict?[11]

The doctrine of the three orders, envisaged as sets of
objects and presupposing separate faculties giving access
to them, seems to be for Pascal a great *évidence*, an enor-
mously important three-pronged intuition about the universe. Bodies, minds, hearts, to which he adds God, of
course: these great illuminating ideas have for him on the
scale of his entire undertaking the role played by terms like
number, space, movement, and time, in the limited

perspective of science and geometry. They are par excellence his first principles, and over them his powers of feeling and knowing range continually, now repeating the
distinction and stressing those things that are proper to its
branches, now showing how questions arising on a lower
plane, insoluble in their own restricted terms, are answer-
able if viewed from above, and in a system. The parts of his
vision are separate, of course; but they have their logic:
they imply, reinforce, and evoke each other.

Derivation of the Orders

We are now in a position to comment on the origins and
nature of the distinction between the three orders and on
its relevance to fragments other than those in which it appears openly. As for origins in the sense of sources, the
possibilities are endless, blending into a philosophical and
theological tradition that takes us back to the Greeks and to
the Bible, via Saint Augustine, Cicero, and Epictetus. (I am
not forgetting, of course, Pascal's contemporary and intellectual rival, Descartes, nor the milieu of Port-Royal.) In
treating such a vast question it would be hard to avoid
reducing precise statements to commonplaces. Of more
interest here is the proximate derivation of the orders that
may be seen in the very text of the *Pensées*. As leading
elements in the thought of Pascal, they do not spring out of
the blue, but depend on prior and more basic notions. He
says in the *liasse* entitled "Ordre" that the means of persuasion or the proofs on which he will rely will come from
two sources, Nature and Scripture, but the orders no less
than the proofs stem from these two terms. By examining
them and their successive branchings we may recover the
basis, immanent in Pascal's ways of thinking and of posing
problems, on which this powerful triad rests. He
assumes—he does not postulate, for what he takes as
granted is self-evident and not a matter of convention—

that nature is not one but two; it is composed of bodies and souls ("corps" and "âmes"). Then, if one focuses one's attention on the soul, that term shows itself to be two, in turn: mind and heart ("esprit" and "coeur"). Although the table is blurred somewhat by the active presence in Pascalian psychology of notions that are ultimately philosophical, such as sense, imagination, will, memory, there is no doubt that the parts of the soul that count most for Pascal are the two mentioned. One may then go on to recognize the duplicity of the heart. Sometimes, as the seat of the affections and passions, it turns toward things, people, and pleasures, showing the face of *concupiscence;* sometimes it turns inward and upward toward purity and insight, and then it enters the regime of *charité*. With this last division in the series developed from "Nature" the three orders come into being. Of course, there are really four levels instead of three in the background of Pascal's thought. The fourth one—that of a hidden but partly accessible God—comes out of the term opposite Nature, which is Scripture. With body, mind, heart, and God as derivatives from Nature and what stands above Nature, Pascal has the conceptual equipment he needs.

The logical procession that ends in the concept of orders accounts for the peculiar force of the scheme. The secret lies in the quality of the distinctions, in the relation that creates them. "Nature:" versus "Scripture" exhausts in its way all the possibilities in the universe, for it establishes a dichotomy. Facing us as we start to think about the problems of apologetics are these two factors, and everything not included in one falls in the other. We begin with things and a book. And again, as we go down the branching line that leads to body, mind, and heart, at each fork we have (or are supposed to have, I believe) the same sense of exhaustiveness: in their particular domains the pairs *âme/corps, coeur/esprit, charité/concupiscence* divide up restricted but whole territories just as satisfactorily as the original distinction covered the entire universe of things and discourse.

Pascal's conception of the three orders has its origin in his way of posing the apologetic problem as the reconciliation of Nature and Scripture, and it has special force as an apparently exhaustive way of dividing up the world and the self. The framework and the lower-level terms that result are ruled by a logic of analogy. I have referred earlier to this point; we can now see more clearly what the technique means and implies. It is true that Pascal prides himself on using untechnical language that grows out of common experience; but it is no less true that he bends both the meanings and the ambiguities of common usage to his own purposes (as does any original thinker or writer); he takes them up into a process that regulates or regularizes them. Actually the process is going on at all times in the *Pensées*, but it becomes especially noticeable in the fragments concerning order.

Here is how the method works beneath the surface of the text. The same words (as, for example, "éclat," "grandeurs," "victoire") take on different meanings or references—not by equivocation but by analogy—as the center of attention shifts up and down the series of orders; and those same words may form chains of proportions as one moves across the board, so to speak (as when Pascal tells us what is on each level, who is able to recognize its realities, and who the great representatives are, and what comes about as a result of their labors); and, again, those same words are subject to negative or positive coloration according to whether they are in the preparatory phase of Pascal's argument—that of *l'homme sans Dieu*, or in its concluding, reconciling phase, that of *l'homme avec Dieu* (or, to take up the language of fragment 933, whether everything on the three levels isolates itself from God or orients itself toward him). Love, once bad, as concupiscence, is transformed into charity; the mind, once proud and hostile, humbles itself in the wager; the body, once an obstacle, cooperates in Christian conduct; Nature, which once stood alone, emerges as creation; and Scripture, full of opposed *dicta* and obscurities, opens up to the gaze of the seeker when interpreted correctly. All these radical changes would seem arbitrary if there were no regular process of argument supplied to warrant them; and the clearest expression, in my opinion, of the framework that regulates the discourse is precisely the table of orders as distinguished, first, and then interrelated by Pascal. He has been called the Christian Socrates, and here the comparison has more than general significance, for the three orders with God presiding over all suggest the passage in the *Republic* in which Socrates invites his hearers to join him in discourse based on a divided line over which the Idea of Good stands as the last cause and end.

Variations and Applications

The triple distinctions of the orders is, more than any other device, the key to his universe of discourse, and indeed, its importance goes beyond discourse, since it concerns discontinuities in being. But he does not use it mechanically. In its most complete version it emerges at a critical point in the argument—among the "preuves de Jésus-Christ"— with great clarity and force. Once we have it before us, we can trace out Pascal's way of approximating it elsewhere, or using it in a reduced form, or subdividing one or another of the domains. First let us look at two of the subdivisions. In fragment 511 Pascal distinguishes between two kinds of *esprit droit*, one of them being the *esprit de justesse* (capable of drawing many consequences from a few principles, as in the study of the effects or the behavior of water), the other being the *esprit de géométrie* (capable of working with a large number of principles without confusing them). This is a specification of mental gifts: we are on the second of the three levels. A related fragment develops the famous contrast of *esprit de géométrie* and *esprit de finesse*. This is again the level of mind, though as we have seen, there is good reason to stress the affinities of *finesse* and the working of the heart.[12] Pascal's vocabulary combines words drawn from both intellectual and sentimental registers. The language of proving shows itself in the references to principles and reason, and yet the insistent use of the verb "sentir," the noun "sentiment," and the adjective "immédiat" alert us to the presence of feeling and of total reactions to total situations.

Sometimes, instead of making distinctions within one order, Pascal calls into play a limited version of his broad scheme, as in fragment 199 (on the two infinites of Nature, the disproportion of man the problem of knowledge). In the sequence of his thought there we find a brilliant example of the uses to which the lower two levels of the three orders may be put. The body of man takes on an intermediate size when compared first to stellar space and objects and then to what we would now call microscopic and submicroscopic reality. This leads the way to a better understanding of mind and its situation (the dualism is very plain at this point): just as the body lies between extremes of physical size in a position impossible to locate exactly, since the extremes are infinitely distant from it, so the mind has in the universe of intelligible beings an intermediate capacity that enables it to deal with truths proportional to it but never to grasp first principles and last conclusions. But that is only one effect that Pascal draws from the opposition of orders. We cannot really know things in the middle region of physical and intellectual things, because to know them truly would require knowledge of the extremes. We cannot understand the parts without knowing the whole, and Pascal has already asserted that that is inaccessible. Having administered that bit of humiliation to man in his efforts to know, Pascal asks how we, being two, can ever know physical things, which are one. How can body-mind establish a "proportion" to body alone? And he takes the further step of denying the possibility that mind by itself will ever know the other kind of substance. It falls into confusion and error, because it tends to assign mental qualities to bodies or corporeal qualities to minds.[14] Finally, in the coup de grâce for our pretensions to knowledge, he turns on man's efforts to understand himself and asks the question that haunts every such dualism: how can we ever grasp the union of body and mind that is our nature? That is the final disproportion: he begins in fragment 199 by aligning bodies—our body and other bodies, large and small; that leads to a confrontation of two orders out of the three; and we end with something very like the statement at the opening of fragment 308 to the effect that there is an infinite distance from bodies to minds. Actually the notion of infinite regulates all these disproportions. Finite body cannot overcome the distance between itself and infinite body, nor can mind overcome the infinite distance between its order and that of body.

In the line of doing and morality, as well as in knowing, we find striking examples of the way in which two of the orders may be played against each other. The oppositions take various forms. The order of force is allied (forcibly) with that of justice; the mind that knows beauty contends with the *fort* and neither can score against the other except by tyranny (which is Pascal's name for the attempt to universalize the quality proper to one order, so that other orders come under its sway, or, in other words, to make someone accept a disproportion as if it were a proportion); the order of *divertissement*, where concupiscence pursues distracting things or people, contrasts with that of the mind, and serious introspection; the strength arising from knowledge in the sciences is of no avail in times when consolation is needed, when *morale* is appropriate; the view that the *peuple* has of society, its uses and charades

and hierarchies, differs essentially from that of the true
Christian, who can see all that in a higher light; reason has
its terrain that is distinct from that of *volonté*; mind is bound
to yield on principles and on knowledge of spiritual things
to the heart; proofs of any kind in matters of morality and
religion need the cooperation of the Machine; Nature must
be completed by Scripture; when one interprets the Bible,
the letter conveys a meaning to the mind, of course, but in
the Old Testament it must serve as a means to the ways of
the spirit and of figuration; in studying the history of the
Jews, Pascal would be helpless without the distinction between the *juifs charnels* and the *juifs spirituels*. In all these
and in other examples, the tension between orders, with
the implied necessity of seeing the lower in the terms of the
higher, and, for that matter, of understanding the higher in
terms of the lower, imparts interest and characteristic life
to Pascal's thought and style.

It would be possible to explore further logical, metaphysical, and theological aspects of the three orders. Let us not,
however, neglect its implications for human personality. It
fixes the outlines of what might be called the char-
acterology of Pascal. Through the workings of Pascal's
dramatic imagination, crowds of people, good and bad,
great and small, come into view in the *Pensées*. From evoca-
tions of their observable behavior he moves on, taking us
with him, into their inner life, where they sort themselves
out into moral types, such as *charnels*, *génies*, *saints*. Taken
together they constitute one of the great structural facts of
this Apology. I mean that what Pascal's rhetorical problem
involves is at least three persons. There is (1) the apologist,
(2) the person for whom he writes or with whom he talks,
and (3) some person or persons behaving in a characteristic
fashion and furnishing material for the comments of the
other two.[14] It may be that, to be complete, we should add
a fourth person to the situation, the actual reader, as opposed to the imagined reader whom Pascal sees as his

target. In any case the social types who come into sight, thanks to the criteria furnished by the distinction of the three orders, become actors on the scene of the world with whom he concerns himself. He had already tried something similar, in the first ten *Lettres provinciales*; he knew that the formula would work from the success he had had with (1) "Louis de Montalte," (2) the "Provincial de ses amis," and (3) the theologians engaged in the controversy over Arnauld and Jansenism. These last provide a dramatic focus of interest and source of fascination for the observers, one of whom points out for the benefit of the other what the Jansenists' opponents are doing, often unwittingly, and what the *raisons des effets* are.[15]

There is one last point to be noted here. Every man is a composite; no man belongs purely and simply to one or another of the domains or orders; everyone has the same fundamental set of capabilities and tendencies. Classifying men into types merely draws attention to dominant inclinations. The case is like that of the theory of humors. All four humors are present in each of us to some degree; but the proportions of the ingredients vary, and that variation determines the type to which we belong. And so the three orders yield *caractères* in a sense of that word that Molière or La Bruyère would have understood at once.

Convergence of Two Senses of "Ordre"

Sorting people into relatively static classes is in the end less interesting to Pascal than causing them to move out of their characters and to undertake, as individuals, a spiritual itinerary. We may now rejoin, after a detour for the purpose of isolating principles and their consequences, the main line of Pascal's argument. Those who live on one or the other of the first two levels of sense and mind (or reason) must be motivated to take themselves in hand and redirect their powers and desires. Gradually the attractive force of the hierarchical arrangement makes itself felt, and the propriety of subordinating what is lower on the scale to what stands above it. From the point of view of the person leading the discussion and composing the proofs, being purely or mainly a *charnel* or a *génie* is not enough, is intolerable, in fact—and not just for the apologist. The person addressed will come to know in time that his situation is unbearable, unless he is destined to be one of those negative example figures who, willy-nilly and in their indirect way, confirm the thesis of man's corruption. To live mainly on either of the first two levels is inevitably to neglect and misunderstand the two that are left. That is how tyranny begins: one order attempts to make itself universal at the expense of the others. One might say that Pascal is trying for another kind of universality, in which every order gets its due. He wants to achieve that happy result by means of a progression so conceived that no term following another term cancels the one that precedes it, but elevates it, harmonizes it with the whole. Such a progression traverses all orders, going from unexamined life according to the flesh to insight into the predicament of that strange creature, man, and then to readiness for further evolution onto a level of existence where the heart opens itself to divine inspiration. That moral trajectory eliminates only the inessential; it saves everything worthwhile. And Pascal thinks that progression to be possible for anyone who reads his Apology. At this point then the two meanings of *ordre*—as succession and as hierarchy of domains—converge. In a real sense the two lines of analysis turn into one. The indifferent or hostile *honnête homme*, to be jarred into a sense of the opposed tendencies in his and man's nature, who is pulled away from his amusements and changed into a *chercheur*, and who seeks first the advice of the philosophers, only to see his problems become fixed and impossible to solve; who then can plausibly turn to a survey of religions that would lead him to a sympathetic inquiry into the meaning of the Scriptures: what is such a man doing, if not moving up the ladder defined by the three orders?

The Means of Belief

In his quest for certainty, which must ultimately be religious, Pascal recognizes three means or instruments of belief: *raison, coutume, inspiration.* In his practice, as analyzed in the preceding pages, he makes use of reason in proof and proofs, in order and orders. Certainty depends, first, on clarity in defining and using terms, clarity that gives us the sense of exhaustive distinctions being drawn as the points of departure for the discourse. Pascal takes pains to meet this condition in many instances, no doubt, but most decisively in the doctrine of the three orders, which are the origins and ends of both logical movement and personal change. Second, certainty depends on a regular flow of discourse, governed by principles and a clear conception of method. Very strong in this area, with the geometrical model in the back of his mind as the term of comparison, Pascal chooses a basically dialectical procedure built on conflicts and resolutions rather than on a linear succession of antecedents and consequents. Working in the light of that basic mode, he adjusts the stages of his presentation to his reader's evolution, creating thus a fusion of dialectic and rhetoric. The latter is subordinated to the former, for rhetoric is not, in the thought of Pascal, an autonomous and indifferent discipline with operations allowable apart from philosophical and religious truths.[16] The fragment (298) treating the order of the heart as opposed to that of the mind offers an important sign of this adjustment. Since the heart must be moved rather than simply instructed, the rigor of strictly logical argument—impossible to realize, anyway, because of the subject matter—will be tempered in a flexible, digressive way of exposition. Everything needed in a morality of conversion will be assembled and unified by reference to an end that is always present. In the third place, certainty depends on achieving the right texture of discourse. Here Pascal's intellectual inventions are many and ingenious. He adduces a vast number of proofs or inferences in matters of detail, some based on thinking by syllogism, others on quasi-mathematical forms of reasoning, others on particular instances of tensions resolved with the help of synoptic principles, and still others on divine intervention and efficacy. Orders, methods, proofs: these are guarantees of certainty that are found by reason and directed to reason. And yet all this rational effort, though necessary and effective in its way, will never suffice. It must be completed by the Machine and by divine inspiration. The light reason sheds will never have the stability and immediacy required for conviction if it exists apart from the other two means.

3 | Fixation of Belief

Elements,
Tendencies,
and Habits

Leaving the area of proof, order, and mind, we arrive at the second of the three "moyens de croire": *coutume.* It, too, is a way to certainty and to the security of faith, but it builds on another side of our being.

> Il faut donc faire croire nos deux pièces, l'esprit par les raisons [*var.* démonstration] qu'il suffit d'avoir vues une fois dans sa vie et l'automate par la coutume, en ne lui permettant pas de s'incliner au contraire. (Fr. 821)

What is that second *pièce*? The reference to the automaton (one thinks at once of the fragments in which Pascal mentions the role of the *Machine,* a word that seems to be synonymous with *automate*) suggests the body. The body now appears to be about to come somehow into its own, after the uncompromising intellectualism that colors the arguments in many of the texts. Here it is important to make some distinctions and to see some interrelations. By elimination and comparison we can come close, at least, to

understanding the meanings that animate Pascal's fluid
and often ambiguous vocabulary. Take *corps,* for example.
One sense or application we can set aside at once. That is
the notion of body as an organism formed of interdepen-
dent members, though this kind of body is implied or
explicit in many significant passages. Pascal may refer to
the body of the Church (fr. 967), or of an army (fr. 421), or
of an institution (the *parlement* in fr. 706), or of discourse
(fr. 696), or of a mite (fr. 199)—to mention only a few
examples. Perhaps the most important usage here concerns the Church as a body of "membres pensants" (fr.
372) united by one spirit in God; to this body corresponds
by negative analogy the "corps de réprouvés" (fr. 957).
That this organic conception of body is essential to the
Apology may be seen at once if one recalls the two critical
moments in religious conversion: the first, an individual
experience, when one returns to God from an existence
centered on oneself, and the second, a collective experience, as one becomes a part, a conscious member, of the
body composed of all faithful people.

All of that turns on the fact that Pascal sets up two terms,
body and limbs, in a special relationship and uses them in
a régime of discourse that is sometimes literal, sometimes
figurative. As important as it is, this image and this idea
give way to and are integrated into the basic dualism of
Pascal's thought. Again, fragment 821 may serve as a starting point for us: "Nous sommes automate autant qu'esprit." One would infer from this passage that our two parts
or pieces are *esprit* and *corps,* at least when the theme of
knowing dominates. The mind knows, the body does not.
But this pair easily changes back and forth with *âme* and
corps, whenever the context is broader and activities other
than knowing—such as feeling, willing, or simply
being—are relevant. And we must not forget the place of
cœur: perhaps the most satisfactory rule of thumb for

understanding Pascal on this point is to think of body as opposed to soul, and soul as susceptible of division into two parts—mind and heart—that have related functions, thinking and feeling. We rejoin the theme of the three orders, which seems, indeed, to be the most developed form of the underlying dualism.[1] Of course, at appropriate moments Pascal has additions to make to this vocabulary, such as sense, imagination, memory, and will, thus enriching it with borrowings from the lexicon of philosophical psychology. Here, as before, we must resist the temptation to freeze the distinctions and definitions, because in fact they interconnect and overlap. Pascal's terminology shows its rigor when that is needed, but it seems to thrive on a certain imprecision; the key words refer less to objects than to areas with shifting boundaries.

Automate and *Machine* connote, then, the other substance, *corps*.[2] As we study the fragments where these words occur, it is obvious that change and abstraction have taken place. What happens to them reminds us of the change and widening of sense undergone by *cœur*. If we consider for a moment Descartes and his way of treating *cœur* in the *Traité des passions de l'âme,* we can see what is happening to the word. For him it is a purely mechanical organ, a kind of heater responsible for the movement of the blood and its circulation; in his mind it has none of the technical and special moral sense so notable in the *Pensées*, where Pascal takes as his base the tradition of biblical and Christian morality.[3] From the Cartesian point of view, Pascal has transferred the heart from the category of extended substance to that of thinking substance. I have been able to find only one instance in the *Pensées* of the word "cœur" used in its literal sense:

Diversité.
La théologie est une science, mais en même temps combien est-ce de sciences? Un homme est un suppôt,

> mais si on l'anatomise, que sera-ce? La tête, le cœur,
> l'estomac, les veines, chaque veine, chaque portion de
> veine, le sang, chaque humeur de sang. (Fr. 65)

Even here the heart and the other parts of the body are
indicators of something else, the divisions of theology.
Elsewhere the heart is not an organ but a power and a
tendency concerned with feeling, action, and insight, and
regularly understood in opposition to the mind.

A like shift occurs in the uses of the words for "body"
and "machine." They leave the register of physical things
and take on moral significance. Again, one can point to
examples where the literal sense is intended:

> La machine d'arithmétique fait des effets qui ap-
> prochent plus de la pensée que tout ce que font les
> animaux; mais elle ne fait rien qui puisse dire qu'elle a de
> la volonté comme les animaux. (Fr. 741)

And yet Pascal, as before, pushes the literal sense of the
word (it designates a physical apparatus) in the direction of
thought, and pursuing this idea, notes the absence of desire or will. He moves the physical object into a discussion
that is psychological and moral; he tests the validity of his
dualism by looking at a case on the borderline.[4] Writing of
Descartes, Pascal gives the term a metaphysical sense:

> Il faut dire en gros: cela se fait par figure et mouve-
> ment. Car cela est vrai, mais de dire quelles et composer
> la machine, cela est ridicule. Car cela est (faux) inutile et
> incertain et pénible. (Fr. 84, variant)

Here we encounter the *machine du monde* and the sphere of
quantitative realities that have been promoted and transformed into universal principles of explanation and con-
struction. But Pascal continues to see things from his own
angle. Even when the literal sense of machine has been so
obviously left behind, as in the speculation of Descartes,

Pascal turns the train of our thought in another direction: "Et quand cela serait vrai, nous n'estimons pas que toute la philosophie vaille une heure de peine" (fr. 84).

This movement away from a limited understanding of body and in particular of machine comes to light very near the beginning of the *Pensées*, a fact that is not without significance, for Pascal seems intent on introducing not systematically but succinctly all the terminology necessary for his apologetic argument. In fragment 7 of the *liasse* entitled "Ordre" he notes that faith is a gift of God, whereas proof is a product of man; proof may serve as a means or instrument, but faith is finally a matter of the heart, of *credo* and not *scio*. The first line of the fragment reads: "Lettre qui marque l'utilité des preuves. Par la machine." Whether one accepts that punctuation—the period after *preuves*, as fixed by Lafuma—or not, in favor of reading the line as a single unit, as Brunschvicg and Chevalier do, it is clear (moderately so!) that the Machine is connected in some way with proofs and with the human aspects of conversion. Fragment 5 evokes a friend who is about to give up the search and mentions a letter of exhortation that might be written, urging him to continue. The friend would be happy to find some light; he has tried, but as he says, "Rien ne paraît." And without any light, why search or believe? His belief would be of no use. "Et à cela lui répondre: La Machine." In other words: continue, go on acting *as if*. The problem resembles the one that arises at the end of the fragment on the wager, when the interlocutor says, "Je ne puis croire," and the apologist counsels him to go through the motions; the time for light and assurance will come later.

Obviously the body, as the opposite of mind or soul, is not all that is involved here. In fact, the obstacle to understanding what Pascal means to say in the treatment of the second *moyen de croire* may very well arise from the tendency we have to think of the Machine as a part rather than

as a whole. Is it not the whole person and his total behavior, his entire mode of conduct that is at issue here? We
should not think of body or soul or mind or heart, but
rather about all these aspects of the human being, about
powers of thought, feeling and action (1) insofar as they
are capable of habitation, of being bent in new directions
(such is the positive note in the definition of "machine"),
and (2) insofar as they do their work in the absence of valid
reasons, or explicit or deliberate thought or desire (that is
the negative aspect of *machine*). The context and argument
in which *automate, machine,* and *coutume* have a place in the
search for faith is one in which man acquires habits or acts
according to them. What interests Pascal here is the whole
person as a creature of habit.

> La coutume de voir les rois accompagnés de gardes, de
> tambours, d'officiers et de toutes les choses qui ploient la
> machine vers le respect et la terreur fait que leur visage,
> quand il est quelquefois seul et sans les accompagne-
> ments imprime dans leurs sujets le respect et la terreur,
> parce qu'on ne sépare point dans la pensée leurs per-
> sonnes d'avec leurs suites qu'on y voit d'ordinaire
> jointes. (Fr. 25)

These lines affirm the teachability of the human subject
and the fact that, once taught, he will respond according
to the inculcated pattern. Moreover, the learned behavior
is not without a kind of judgment and mental activity.

> Et le monde qui ne sait pas que cet effet vient de la cou-
> tume, croit qu'il vient d'une force naturelle. Et de là
> viennent ces mots: le caractère de la divinité est empreint
> sur son visage, etc. . . . (Fr. 25)

The mind is not inactive; it thinks it has the explanation for
the respect and terror; and it is right in that it sees real
effects but wrong in that it assigns them to an illusory
cause (the "force naturelle"). Pascal is composing another

variation on the theme of finding *la raison des effets,* a constantly renewed exercise at which he thought himself quite adept, much more so than *le peuple* or *le monde.* Everything we have been sorting out is present in these two passages: emotional reactions, judgment, speech, overt behavior, the process of habituation and its results. Custom, the second means of belief, is directed not to the mind alone nor to the heart nor to the body—those would be incomplete addresses—but to the person as a whole who is an ensemble of powers subject to learning and fixation, not a mechanical collection of parts.

The Habit of Obedience

The *Pensées* assume that readers are subjects capable of receiving predicates and qualities. Without that supposition the work would make no sense whatever. And once we see that man, the whole of man, is the subject of custom, we can understand better than before the nature and limits of proofs. The mind, which is the subject of proofs, is only a part. As we study the second means, we witness a great widening of focus in the argument. Pascal would never have said that "la raison peut tout," but in fragment 517 he reports and accepts Montaigne's statement that "la coutume peut tout." We can best investigate the nature and works of custom, and its relation to proof and faith, by studying a group of contexts or perspectives (with the zones of reality that correspond to them) in which custom has the role of decisive principle. In this way it will be possible to build up a picture of custom as a cooperating force in apologetics, staying always close to specific passages and paying attention to the peculiarities of Pascal's reasoning. It may also be possible to explain why he accepts so easily Montaigne's hyperbolic statement.

Current usage in both English and French tends to distinguish between custom and habit as learned patterns of behavior that are shared by the members of a group or found in individuals, respectively. A strict separation along those lines was not common in seventeenth-century French. "Coutumes" is applied to the habits of people taken singly as well as to those of a collectivity. Nevertheless, for our purposes, there is reason for starting with that distinction and treating the textual data accordingly. In the apologetic portion of the *Pensées*, at least, Pascal concentrates on individuals rather than groups and on the certainties that will bring them to particular acts of conversion.

Fragment 25 has already described the relationship between the king and his subjects and shown the origins of custom and its compelling force once established. Fragments 88 and 89 continue the same line of thought, apropos of the respect accorded to persons "de grande naissance" and of great wealth. Of course these concrete examples are based on a general and fundamental thesis. In fragment 60 Pascal goes to the heart of the matter. The source of justice is not to be found in nature (and the natural law thought to be its sequel) or in reason or in the legitimate authority of a lawmaker or king, but in custom, which is caprice and usurpation entrenched and fortified. As a system of prescriptive usages its essence is to be received, to be taken for granted; it has a mystical authority all its own. When in his reflections Pascal expresses this view of justice, he reaches almost the highest level of awareness possible on the subject: he (and we) have seen through the appearances to the oppressive reality of human justice. One further step remains: to recognize that this is the best we can hope for since the fall of man. Custom brings order and prevents revolt. However, it will not do for *le peuple* to have this insight. The wise legislator for Pascal's body politic, like his counterpart in Plato's *Republic,* knows that the people have to be deceived at times and especially to be kept in the dark about the origins of things.

Fragment 525 modifies the argument slightly and carries it to its last stage. The absence of justice or reason behind custom is reasserted, but Pascal adds that, since people will not accept subjection unless it is reasonable or just, they must be left with the illusion that custom has something of those qualities. Otherwise they will rebel.

From the foregoing examples and analyses certain conclusions may be drawn. (1) In the thought of Pascal the notion of custom has complicated and paradoxical relations with a number of important terms like *nature, reason, chance, force;* we shall have more to say about this semantic complex later. (2) Custom serves to legitimize and reinforce something considerably less than what is true or reasonable. (3) Custom may be taken as an end, as an ultimate value or state, but it is essentially the means to an end. (4) It comes into its own where a hierarchical order is to be established, one in which inferior ranks are to be clearly set off from superiors. (5) In such a situation its function is precisely to overcome resistance to order and to bring men into conformity with that order; it stabilizes and maintains the hierarchy by creating a habit of obedience. These statements apply directly to the life of groups within the framework of society, but they apply just as well to the inner lives of individuals, if we make the small adjustments needed to set up a valid proportion.[5]

Custom stabilizes but is in itself unstable. Latching onto an ancient theme here, Pascal borrows skeptical commonplaces from a line of thought that goes back to the Pyrrhonians (and to the Greek Sophists before them). One of the most notable things about customs, habits, laws, is that they vary from place to place and change from time to time. The causes of this instability lie in the weakness of human nature and the capriciousness of corrupted reason. Neither lasting order nor real uniformity (two decidedly positive values in Pascal's axiology) has ever come from such bases—with one quite significant exception in the history of the Jews. They founded and kept alive through many vicissitudes a rigorous code that goes back to a time and place near the beginning of history. The explanation is that their laws and customs had a divine rather than a human origin.

Custom and Doing

We have already observed that, although we tend now both in French and English to use the words "coutume" and "custom" for phenomena that are mainly collective, the connection with habit in the area of individual behavior is quite strong. Even with individuals something of the notion of a group remains, for Pascal often thinks in terms of types and instances of types. The group is then composed of the members belonging to a type; this is something different from what comes to mind when we think of a social order, made up of distinct sorts and conditions of men who work together or at least share a common existence in relative peace. Custom now appears in three important areas: (1) *doing*, where it affects the choice of one's métier; (2) *thinking*, where it stands behind one's everyday opinions; and (3) *believing*, where it plays a role in one's religious faith.

Pascal takes up the diverse callings to which men have devoted themselves, mentioning three in particular—those of masons, soldiers, and roofers—but referring also to "toutes les conditions des hommes" (fr. 634). A choice is involved here, the most important choice in one's life. By what is it determined? By chance, he answers: "Le hasard en dispose." But it becomes clear that chance is the occasion and cause of custom, for chance happenings, when repeated, institute custom. The brief analysis contained in this fragment shows us in action the process that leads to the choice of vocation. Again and again, in a way that is neither deliberate nor planned, the child hears judgments, value judgments, regarding *métiers*.

C'est un excellent couvreur, dit-on, et en parlant des soldats: ils sont bien fous, dit-on, et les autres au contraire: il n'y a rien de grand que la guerre, le reste des hommes ne sont que des coquins. (Fr. 634)

In this situation things heard bring about the decision. "A force d'ouïr louer en l'enfance ces métiers et mépriser tous les autres, on choisit." That is not quite the whole story, however. The rival term, *nature*, is never far from *coutume*, and nature or a kind of natural instinct enters into the choice. We love naturally virtue and hate naturally folly, and the judgments of praise or blame, when applied to trades or callings direct our instinct, providing it with specific objects by which it may be satisfied. There is some seesawing in the thought of fragment 634: whereas nature makes only men, custom has such strength that it makes all the conditions of men; and yet, as we see in the last lines of the text, in spite of the constraint imposed on it by custom, nature sometimes wins out, keeping man in his instinct against all habituation. It seems that here, at least, Pascal reaches for a compromise and for cooperation between these two factors in human life. In this context, by strengthening an opinion about what is worth while and what is not, custom brings about an ordering of our powers and a stable decision as to what we are to do with ourselves. The opinion is irrational, but with the backing of habit it suffices for the most important thing of all in life. Already the temptation is irresistible: one feels obliged to ask whether the outline of this analysis applies not only to what is important in this life, but also to what is most important *tout court*.

Some Nonrational Thinking

If we turn from callings to ways of thinking, from acts backed by custom to opinions and what stands behind them, we usually find in the relevant fragments a particular proposition or the trace of a proposition, and somewhere nearby an explanation of how it gets its force. Sometimes, however, Pascal speaks in general of "principes naturels." A curious example in fragment 44 will serve as an introduction. After telling us of the misdeeds of imagination for several paragraphs, he moves on to other sources of error, one of which is the senses. He imagines someone who asserts that a vacuum is possible, that such a thing as a *vide* can be, and then this view is denounced by someone else as an illusion of the senses due to the working of custom. The fundamental truth that Pascal means to illustrate is that any principle, no matter how natural it may seem, can be made to appear false. He happens to believe, as we know from elsewhere, that the principle in question here is true; the interesting thing is that in order to discredit it he has someone criticize it as an "illusion des sens fortifiée par la coutume." The choice of words in this brief formula seems almost perfect as an indication of the way in which custom and habit work.

In the middle of the discussion of Pyrrhonianism and dogmatism (fr. 131), we find a reference to the evidence— "impressions de la coutume, de l'éducation, des mœurs des pays et les autres choses semblables"—which the dogmatists, who think that it is possible to know with certainty and that they do have some such knowledge, use in fact as the basis of their assertions. No specific propositions emerge from this passage. Pascal says simply that foundations like these are upset by the least breath of the Pyrrhonians. Look into their works, he says; if one is not already persuaded, one soon will be, and perhaps too much so!

In fragments 125 and 126 the contest between nature and custom becomes explicit, and it is an unequal battle. There is the bald affirmation that our natural principles are our accustomed ones. We receive them from our parents in the way that animals learn to hunt from their parents. In the first of the two fragments there is no attempt to be more

specific about these "principes naturels." Pascal hurries on
to an elaborate verbal figure, to the effect that custom ef-
faces nature, though some nature is ineradicable by custom; but then again some custom that is against nature
cannot be eradicated by nature or by another custom.
Fragment 126 shows by an example what he seems to have
in mind:

> Les pères craignent que l'amour naturel des enfants ne
> s'efface. Quelle est donc cette nature sujette à être ef-
> facée?

His answer brings more paradoxical word play:

> La coutume est une seconde nature qui détruit la pre-
> mière. Mais qu'est-ce que nature? Pourquoi la coutume
> n'est-elle pas naturelle? J'ai grand peur que cette nature
> ne soit elle-même qu'une première coutume, comme la
> coutume est une première nature.

The implied proposition is: "Les enfants aiment leurs
pères"; but something like its contrary, "Les enfants peuvent ne pas aimer leurs pères," is true or at least plausible
given the power of habit and custom. And so by this
example, rather than show us how a natural principle is
fortified by custom (to the point that its natural force
evaporates), Pascal imagines a situation where a principle
running counter to nature may be so strengthened as to
replace the instinctive tendency.

Since custom fortifies sense impressions (the case of the
vide), and since custom modifies nature or a natural instinct
(the case of the love that children have for their parents), it
is obvious that Pascal tends strongly to reduce nature to
custom or to make it, as a principle, dependent on custom.
Another aspect of the human makeup remains, the mind
or reason. And here, too, we find something quite similar.
In fragment 821, where he stresses the weakness of demonstration based on reasoning, two propositions that ex-

press two everyday beliefs receive attention, namely that tomorrow will come, and that we shall all die. What is more strongly believed than these two, asks Pascal. And yet those beliefs do not rest on rational or logical proofs. It is custom, habit, repeated experiences that have left their trace in our minds and given an air of certainty to these beliefs. In fragment 882 the contrast between what reason can do and what custom can do is made even clearer. Pascal formulates two theses, puts them into questions, and then applies reason and custom to the problem of finding answers.

> Athées.
> Quelle raison ont-ils de dire qu'on ne peut ressusciter?
> Quel est plus difficile de naître ou de ressusciter, que ce qui n'a jamais été soit, ou que ce qui a été soit encore?
> Est-il plus difficle de venir en être que d'y revenir?

From the point of view of reason, both possibilities are equally acceptable. But one is current and certain, and the other is not.

> La coutume nous rend l'un facile, le manque de coutume rend l'autre impossible.
> Populaire façon de juger.

Whether it is a matter of natural principles that are modified or made to seem wrong, or of strongly held opinions having the form of predictions, custom rather than nature or reasoning provides finally the energy the mind needs to persevere in a judgment. It may be a popular way of thinking—Pascal regularly associates the workings of custom with *le peuple*—but it is an effective way.

Fragment 419 shows us Pascal using the same trump card in a situation where the opposing idea is nature once more. In six lines he states his principle and then applies it in three zones of reality, one of which presents itself in a new and interesting manner.

La coutume est notre nature. Qui s'accoutume à la foi la croit, et ne peut plus ne pas craindre l'enfer, et ne croit autre chose.

Qui s'accoutume à croire que le roi est terrible, etc.

Qui doute donc que notre âme étant accoutumée à voir nombre, espace, mouvement, croit cela et rien que cela.

The allusion to the king and to the reactions felt by his subjects shows us what Pascal appears to take as the typical case of customary behavior and the power of habit. The context suggested by that line is social and political. The sentence that precedes it is very close to the central idea of the present chapter, to be treated in the next section, since it comes last in my series of doing, thinking, and believing as influenced by custom. It states boldly and aphoristically Pascal's thesis concerning the second *moyen de croire*. At this point it is already worthwhile to note the analogy between respect for the king and respect for religion or—why not be more exact?—between terror at the sight of the king and what he might do if offended and terror in the mind of the sinner at the thought of God and punishment in hell. If you accustom yourself to the idea of the king as terrible, he becomes so (we know that from fragment 25); if you acquire the habit of faith, it becomes believable. Perhaps the most surprising idea, however, is contained in the last sentence. "Nombre," "espace," "mouvement" are terms that preside over our contact with the physical world and regulate the physicomathematical science we have of that world. Even there the hand of custom makes itself felt and fixes what the mind will accept (believe) and the limits beyond which it will not go. Pascal does not present this conviction as a matter of self-evidence here, although he uses the word "voir," which suggests an immediate intuition. Two other passages of the *Pensées* treat this matter in an apparently opposed way. The first is the opening of the fragment "Infini-rien":

> Notre âme est jetée dans le corps où elle trouve
> nombre, temps, dimensions, elle raisonne là-dessus et
> appelle cela nature, nécessité, et ne peut croire autre
> chose. (Fr. 418)

No reference there to irrational or nonrational custom. Instead Pascal tells us that the intuitive knowledge we have
of certain principles is exploited by our discursive reasoning power. The other passage is similar; the argument asserts as a fact that the heart as well as the reason knows;
indeed it knows with certainty some things that are prior to
the operations and certainties of reason.

> Car les connaissances des premiers principes: espace,
> temps, mouvement, nombres, sont aussi fermes qu'au-
> cune de celles que nos raisonnements nous donnent, et
> c'est sur ces connaissances du cœur et de l'instinct qu'il
> faut que la raison s'appuie et qu'elle y fonde tout son
> discours. (Fr. 110)

A few lines below Pascal says that we *feel* principles and
draw conclusions ("Les principes se sentent, les propositions se concluent"), and the key words—*sentir* and *se
conclure*—would lead us directly, it seems, to the difference
between the *esprit de finesse* and the *esprit géométrique*,
rather than to a discussion of custom. My own conclusion
is that custom is both relevant and irrelevant to this kind of
knowledge of first principles: irrelevant when one is making a functional distinction between the starting points of
knowledge and the discourse in which they are developed;
relevant when one considers the genesis of the certainty
we feel about those starting points. In any case, it is interesting to note in fragment 419 the connection between
items thought of as based on the heart and the stabilizing
power of custom.

Custom and Belief

Fragment 821, to which we have already referred, provides in fact a résumé of all the givens in the problem of custom, habit, and their effects. Custom and habit appear in a framework of operations and results of *esprit* and of all other human powers on the one hand, and on the other, processes leading to belief, persuasion, and conviction. Custom and habit (the latter being more exact in this fragment, since the argument evokes mainly individual or typically individual experiences) figure as means to the ends of belief and persuasion. Each of us is just as much automaton as mind, and while proofs or demonstrations may convince the mind, they leave other aspects of human nature either untouched or even opposed to what is proved. Custom works to remove these obstacles to firm conviction.[6]

> Il faut acquérir une créance plus facile qui est celle de l'habitude qui sans violence, sans art, sans argument nous fait croire les choses et incline toutes nos puissances à cette croyance, en sorte que notre âme y tombe naturellement. (Fr. 821)

Reasoning is incomplete, even powerless in the face of the irrational sides of our nature. It makes things complicated and difficult for us; habit makes them easy. By a kind of semantico-verbal reflex Pascal associates habit, belief, and nature. "En sorte que notre âme y tombe naturellement": in this fleeting reference to nature we see another example of his desire not only to show the strength of habit and its superiority when compared to reason, but also to state his view that custom determines what is natural, and thus makes our nature. Moreover, habit can work its fixative effect on the result of a single moment of insight, and dispense us thereafter from the necessity of having constantly in our minds the details of a demonstration.

> Il faut donc faire croire nos deux pièces, l'esprit par les raisons qu'il suffit d'avoir vues une fois en sa vie, et l'automate par la coutume, et en ne lui permettant pas de s'incliner au contraire. (Fr. 821)

After that last sentence Pascal adds: *Inclina cor meum deus*. Could he have been thinking of the night of November 23, 1654, when he knew for a time the One in Whom he believed? The immediate context suggests a single experience based on proofs, but the addition of the Latin phrase shows, I think, how easily Pascal's mind makes the transition from reasoning to the idea of a supernatural encounter.

Here we must add an important qualification to the picture of the workings of custom given in fragment 821. So far we have seen it serving to confirm something seen in the mind and to adjust all our powers to an important truth or opinion, so that we soak it up along with its implications. Note Pascal's own language: " . . . nous abreuver et nous teindre de cette créance." As he continues, his language impels us toward a profounder view, in which we can appreciate the astonishing power of initiative that follows as a kind of property from custom.

> Qui a démontré qu'il sera demain jour et que nous mourrons, et qu'y a-t-il de plus cru? C'est donc la coutume qui nous en persuade. C'est elle qui fait tant de chrétiens, c'est elle qui fait les Turcs, les païens, les métiers, les soldats, etc. (Fr. 821)

Before the mind sees a truth that has been demonstrated, custom can bring belief on its own; in fact, there may never be any demonstration at all. This turn in the argument brings home to us the fact that the apologetic part of the *Pensées* is addressed to a very small group of people in comparision with the total number of possible Christians. It is intended for those who want to reason out the status and claims of the Christian religion, and who are willing to follow an elaborate sequence of steps (that includes some meanders) designed first to start them on a faith-seeking line of thought and behavior and then to pass under review for the sake of their mental comfort, the multitude of proofs contained in the Bible.[7]

An unexpected modulation occurs at the very end of fragment 821. It develops further the critique of reason and, at the same time, enriches our understanding of the resonances that the term custom has for Pascal. After drawing a line on his sheet of paper he writes:

> La raison agit avec lenteur et avec tant de vues sur tant de principes, lesquels il faut qu'ils soient toujours présents, qu'à toute heure elle s'assoupit ou s'égare manque d'avoir tous principes présents. Le sentiment n'agit pas ainsi; il agit en un instant et toujours est prêt à agir. Il faut donc mettre notre foi dans le sentiment, autrement elle sera toujours vacillante.

This establishes a link and an analogy between "coutume" and "sentiment"; by implication it evokes the two *esprits* of geometry and *finesse*, and, beyond that, the heart with its nondiscursive, felt certainties.

The Way to Stability

We began this section with the idea of custom as the second *moyen de croire* that comes into its own after the operations of reason. Fragment 821 summarizes partially the relationship between the two. On the basis of all the foregoing we may complete the summary and describe in a general way how they act and interact. In the first place, there are grounds for distinguishing between zones of custom, for there is some oscillation visible in the fragments between the customs of society and the habits of men, between the group and the individual (considered as a moral type apart from political or social qualifiers). In most instances it seems valuable to observe the distinction, as a means of fixing the context in which custom plays its roles.

Against this background, Pascal finds that custom pervades life in all its aspects—in social order, in our occupations, in our thinking, and in our believing. In all those spheres reason leads to the posing of questions. (1) What is just for man in the order that surrounds him? (2) What is good for him in action? (3) What is receivable as opinion or everyday belief, and (4) what is justifiable in religious faith? The probing activity of reason in three of these zones or sets of circumstances shows itself to be mainly negative: destructive and revolutionary, for it removes the illusion of justice and locates the origin of society in usurping violence; frustrating for the sense of satisfaction and rightness in work, for it removes the illusion of correctness and intelligibility in the choice of a *métier*, putting in its place a decision—if it can be called that—stemming from chance; corrosive in matters of accepted opinions, for it removes the illusion of certainty (who does know whether the sun will rise tomorrow?). In all these applications the veils are torn away, so that we may see the want of truth and the hypnotic presence of custom. In the fourth and last application—to the sphere of faith—reason does its work by proving from nature and by Scripture the fact of corruption and the possibility of redemption. It removes intellectual obstacles by argument, and then, passing from *usage* to *soumission*, leaves the field clear for custom, which now appears in a completely different light as a positive source of strength, rather than as negative, opaque, and a source of bafflement. It tames and reorients the powers of soul and body so that divine inclination may have its effect. The common feature of custom in all these places of application seems to lie in this: it provides stability. And without that quality as a minimal ground of behavior and thought, there can be neither peace in society nor peace of mind. The illusions to which custom gives fixity fall, for the most part, under the heading of "Opinions saines du peuple" (a clearly positive formula); and the hypothesis of the wager needs habit to make of it a firm disposition in which men look and wait for truth. By itself reason is too much involved in the general mobility of nature and of human nature to serve as an acceptable basis.

Other Sources of Stability and Determination

As is known, one of the deepest currents in Pascal's thought, as well as one of the most persistent trains of images in it, has to do with the passage from change to permanence, from movement to repose. It is fascinating to see how the three *moyens de croire* emerge, with their characteristic values, from the list of possible sources of certainty and stability and take their high place in Pascal's thought and universe. Reason and custom, together with their tensions and cooperations, have been uppermost in our discussion of the means of believing. They are the first two of three, the third being God. A certain sequence is intended, as reason has its say and then is seconded by custom: that takes care of mind and everything else in the way of human preconditions; that produces a stable tendency or receptiveness to the touch of grace and the inclining of the heart. But Pascal's resort to this triad suggests a question. What lies behind its appearance? Out of what field and ensemble of meanings does it come? the answer depends ulitmately on the framework—quite traditional, even scholastic—of psychological commonplaces that Pascal works with in the *Pensées*. He directs his arguments toward a human nature made up of powers oriented toward proper operations and results. Between the powers or "puissances" and their operations lies a gap, a region where determining factors may intervene, so as to dispose the powers this way or that. Reason, custom or habit, and God are three such interposed causes. Are there others equally immanent in the universe of Pascal?

A quick inspection of the fragments we have been

studying is all that is needed to convince us that such is
the case. A number of other "moyens" or causes or
pressures, all coming to a focus on human powers and de-
flecting them this way or that, may be found in the vicinity
of the three preferred ones. I see at least five others: nature,
art, chance, authority, and violence. These, plus the other
three, make a list of eight which, when taken together,
give us a concise view of the causal lines crisscrossing the
scene that Pascal and his reader look out on. Pursuing the
matter one step further, we can recover something of what
may have been Pascal's insights and reasonings (insofar as
one can reconstruct such things) as certain ones of those
causes drop out of sight or take a place of lesser importance
than that of the main three.

To figure on the final list, it would seem necessary for a
cause to fulfill a single basic condition. Does it have the
power of producing a lasting disposition? The answer will
be yes, if the cause is reducible to reason, custom, or
God—or to something intimately connected with one of
these, so that it may contribute to the desired end. In the
light of these notions let us look at the items on the list.

1. *Nature.* Two main lines of thought present themselves
here. If we think of physical nature as Pascal conceives it,
we are confronted with the infinitely small and the infinitely large and an endless series of proportions. At any
point along this scale from the unattainable *néant* forward,
the object under study will always be at once a colossus
and a mite. There are no fixities; there are only puzzles.
Radical skepticism forces itself upon us at the end of our
reflections, because all of physical nature is body and
homogeneous *masse*, and we, as heterogeneous compos-
ites of mind and body cannot have a correct or certain
relationship to it. Worse than that, we cannot understand
how our minds or souls can manage any contact at all with
bodies or have any knowledge whatsoever of them. If, on
the other hand, we turn to human nature, the result is just

as discouraging. We may, in a sort of *opinion du peuple*, think of our nature as a stable principle of action, growth, and belief, but Pascal has in the pendulum-like swings of his dialectic, in the theme of the *renversement continuel*, and in man's general record of inconstance more than enough ammunition for discrediting human nature as a foundation on which to build—unless, by a bit of dialectical play with terms, he converts, as we have seen him do, nature into custom.

2. *Art*. If we study the neighbors of this word as it appears in our fragments we can see that it is associated in Pascal's mind with intellectual technique and therefore with reason: he tells us that custom persuades *sans art* (fr. 821), and that the *esprit de finesse* works also *sans art*, the contrast being in this case drawn with a geometrical spirit. Art is thus reducible or nearly so to reason; it has the objectivity and the demonstrative strength of reason. But it also shares in the technicality and the complications of reason, as we shall see later.

3. *Chance*. Obviously this factor, however real and effective it may be in redirecting human life and in altering the motions of bodies, cannot yield a steady force in the shaping of principles, attitudes, or moral dispositions. Moreover, it tends, if repeated, to become custom, as is evident from Pascal's fragments on the choice of occupations. In itself and in isolated instances, it does not provide what Pascal is seeking, though if similar chance events happen often enough, they may produce habit or custom, and thus work in the direction characteristic of those causes.

4. *Violence*. Whether it has the form of sporadic or recurrent acts, or whether it is posed as a threat, violence appears in the *Pensées* mainly as something reducible or traceable to political authority; and through the operations of authority its effects come to be active as custom.

5. *Authority*. In the *Pensées* the foundation of human

tice is alleged to be authority, but if we examine this principle carefully (something one must not encourage common people to do, as they might become restive and opt for the "art de fronder") it turns out to be a way of covering usurpation. Thus authority reduces in one direction to violence and in another direction, when prolonged, it is absorbed into custom. Of course, authority in another sense is irreducible and stands over the whole discussion, because it can be divine, and then it has completely positive effects and connotations; it overrides all other types of subordination, since they embody only relative values; and it shows itself in inspiration, the third means of belief.

And so, as nature becomes custom when it is not contradictory, chance produces custom when repeated, authority and its concomitant violence turn into custom, and art takes on the characteristics of demonstration, we can see not only the elaborateness of Pascal's analysis, but also the tendency it has to revert finally to three terms, "esprit," "automate," and "Dieu," that is, to "raison," "coutume," and "inspiration."

These reductive steps are accompained by a process of interiorization. In a movement characteristic of the Pascalian method of posing and solving problems, outer causes give way to inner causes. Chance, violence, and secular authority impinge on us from the outside; in a sense they are all instances of violence and thus incompatible with the kind of conversion that Pascal intends. For that we must look inward, first to mind and to what it can prove demonstratively or probably, and then to habit, which sustains, strengthens, and makes effective the conclusions reached by reasoning. And so our truly important views and inclinations arise from principles within us. The mind at the end of the *pari* sees for itself, and the hearer of the discourse has within him the power to give himself a new custom (that of behaving as if he believed). Inward and upward is the theme here as in Augustine and in the

Platonists; and that sequence shows once more its fruitfulness in the idiosyncratic language of Pascal.

At this level of analysis the two characteristic phases of Pascal's argument as a whole exert their effects on his vocabulary. Everything said in the Apology takes on its particular coloration or value according to whether it occurs in the phase of *l'homme sans Dieu* or in the phase of *l'homme avec Dieu*. This means that the terms studied so far, even "God," may at times have a negative exponent that all but removes their positive connotations. As a result the senses and values of "nature," "art," "chance," "violence," "authority," "reason," "custom," and "God" have to be rethought when one passes the threshold of the régime that emerges under the sign of man-with-God. The new light of that régime mends or heals nature, makes accessible and acceptable the techniques of art, finds an occasion for locating prophetic truth in apparent chance, gives figurative and merciful qualities to violence, renders palatable the demands of authority (as necessary for sinful man in this life or absolutely legitimate if divine and scriptural authority are involved), justifies custom, and puts us in the presence of a God who remains hidden, but less so than before.

One last remark about custom and its status: of all the factors capable of affecting man's behavior and of directing his powers, it is the only one that provides genuine stability in the initial phase of conversion. Without a constant disposition in one's mental and moral life it is not possible to move on to faith.

Opinion as Custom

The view we have of Pascal's position will be incomplete unless we study the notion of opinion. Opinion is, in fact, a species of custom—custom as mental habit, as more or less conscious thought. When explicit or when made so, it takes the form of judgments that tell us how we ordinarily do something or what we usually accept as true. Pascal writes of opinion in the same strong language that he uses in treating custom.

> Je voudrais de bon cœur voir le livre italien dont je ne connais que le titre, qui vaut lui seul bien des livres, dell'opinone [sic] regina del mondo. J'y souscris sans le connaître, sauf le mal s'il y en a. (Fr. 44)

This is not far from the view he attributes to Montaigne—that custom can do anything. And he associates opinion, like custom, with force. Opinion depends on and uses force. The connection with the idea expressed in the title of the Italian book comes through forcibly:

> La force est la reine du monde et non pas l'opinion, mais l'opinion est celle qui use de la force.
> C'est la force qui fait l'opinion. La mollesse est belle selon notre opinion. Pourquoi? parce que qui voudra danser sur la corde sera seul, et je ferai une cabale plus forte de gens qui diront que cela n'est pas beau. (Fr. 554)

One could very well substitute the word "coutume" for "opinion" without changing the sense. The following passage continues the same train of thought and imagery, but adds a significant new associative link—that of opinion with imagination:

> L'empire fondé sur l'opinion et l'imagination règne quelque temps et cet empire est doux et volontaire. Celui de la force règne toujours. Ainsi l'opinion est comme la reine du monde mais la force en est le tyran. (Fr. 665)

But force cannot have the last word in the whole sequence of Pascal's reasoning. Unless it turns into a manifestation of legitimate authority (that of God, in the last resort), its presence and its unbroken reign signify the human frailty and the consequences of Adam's fault, as they work themselves out in society: force is inconsistent with the free gift of self that meets the free gift of another Self at the coming of grace and charity.

Like imagination, opinion is marked by an absence of reason and of valid connection with reality, with what is the case. Here again the analysis is not simple. Opinions fall into different grades.

> Raison des effets.
> Gradation. Le peuple honore les personnes de grande naissance, les demi-habiles les méprisent disant que la naissance n'est pas un avantage de la personne mais du hasard. (Fr. 90)

The classification of opinions continues, from that of the *habiles*, who honor rather than despise the great—though not as the people do, but rather with an *idée de derrière*, an expectation of gaining something for themselves; to that of the *dévots*, who, with more zeal than understanding, scorn those of noble birth, judging by the light of their piety; and finally the view of the *chrétiens parfaits*, who respect those in a high social status by still another and a higher light ("plus intérieure," says Pascal). He concludes: "Ainsi se vont les opinions se succédant du pour au contre selon qu'on a de la lumière." The gradation depends upon the following distinction: opinions may be present in a mind as mental habits without any attempt on the part of the holder to reason them out; or opinions may be thought about or thought out, and in the latter possibility, they may be analyzed (1) incorrectly or (2) correctly on a scale of degrees and accuracy. Pascal likes this kind of sorting out; he obviously enjoys getting beneath appearances and locating the *raison des effets*. Other occurrences of this phrase show that typically, in addition to the true explanation or judgment furnished by Pascal, there is also present, along with the phenomenon which is the occasion for the opinion, at least one other inadequate judgment. To expound the *raison des effets* is not simply to report the discourse of a truth not known before; it invalidates an active error held by someone. (To be exact, the last fragment cited contains four such errors, one for each of the four groups: *peuple, demi-habiles, habiles* and *dévots*.)

Opinion takes its place alongside custom in the list of possible sources of stability drawn up above. That it is intimately related to custom (I have even said that it is a species of custom) is shown by the fact that it has a certain fixity about it (though it is essentially mental), and also by Pascal's way of playing it off against two of the rivals of custom: reason and force. But the thrust of the argument regarding opinion differs from that regarding custom, in that it is exerted less toward justification than toward verification. The central questions are, therefore, "Is the custom just?" and "Is the opinion true?"

The latter question suggests an enormous enlargement of the role that opinion and custom may play in the Apology. From a few example-propositions such as these—belief that the sun will rise tomorrow, that we are going to die, that we owe respect to the king and fear to God, that the wager is reasonable (even *démonstratif*)—we can move to a far ampler conception of what may be held as opinions in the mind and stabilized by the force of habit. Pascal intends to take us from an unexamined ensemble of opinions about man and his fate to the "truth" about human weaknesses, and their causes and cures. He will show us that man is corrupt, that he has a supernatural destiny, and there is a Redeemer. He will present these and many other new propositions, backed by proofs from Nature and Scripture. In other words we shall accede to a new state thanks to the repeated stimulus of proofs and to the repeated acts that follow from them.[8] This comprehensive view of man, with its supporting reasons and consequences, implants in us a new habit of mind and will; it represents for us a great stride away from confused indifference toward clear certainty.

And yet, although Pascal attaches a great deal of importance to the persuasion that he has deployed in manifold and ingenious ways, he knows—and he says so insistently—that his whole edifice of dialectic and rhetoric is relative in value. For his reader or interlocutor it is mere orthodoxy, that is to say, it is rationalized opinion. The seal of truth and the conviction it brings will come not from reason, proofs or actions, but from another source. Apologetic discourse like that envisaged in the *Pensées* stands up better than unexamined and untested beliefs. That is precisely the point; the reader is better off than before, but only relatively so. The real foundation for the new line of thought and action lies elsewhere, and Pascal is now ready to point it out to us.

The relative progress of the reader as a person is nonetheless indispensable, and it is proper to stress here the moral initiative on which it rests. For the interrelations of custom and opinion, their active and passive aspects (since they are produced by repeated action and yet are capable, in turn, of tending to action and of causing action), their negative and positive senses (depending on their place in the sequence of argument), their confusing power of bringing into play factors at once mechanical and mental—all this complexity has to do in large part with the apologist's influence, and is imposed from the outside. It is important to balance the account and to understand that this new habit is also self-given, that back of this custom based on proofs and acts appears the posture of the *chercheur*, which is the result of a choice.[9]

4 | "Ecoutez Dieu"

The People in Question Any search for certainty is a search for a quality of statement or a state of mind. Whether statement or attitude, it cannot be doubted, its validity is obvious, its connection with reality is assured. Of these two possibilities it seems that Pascal, though concerned with the quality of statement, cares more about the inner experience and its result, and about the means of achieving that result. He wants above all to tell us what happens to the searcher as he reaches the end of his path and *finds* something. But he knows that not everyone is looking or searching, and we do well to recall his classification. People fall into three groups: those who are not seeking, those who are, and those who have already found. If we look at these last, we may understand better what is to be expected of the others, for their proper activities consist in part in working toward the characteristic disposition of those who have reached the goal of certainty in faith.

First, we should set aside the *superstiteux*. "La piété est différente de la superstition,"

Pascal writes. Confusion on this point can lead to dire effects.

> Soutenir la piété jusqu'à la superstition, c'est la détruire. Les hérétiques nous reprochent cette soumission superstitieuse: c'est faire ce qu'ils nous reprochent. (Fr. 181)

From the last sentence we get the basic flaw, which is excessive submission. The trouble arises from the excess, of course, for we have learned elsewhere the definitive formula: "Soumission et usage de la raison: en quoi consiste le vrai christianisme" (fr. 167). Second, among those who believe truly, Pascal again has a distinction in mind. Some believe without having read the Testaments, without having seen the proofs; they have an inner disposition that is essentially holy.

> Ceux qui croient sans avoir lu les testaments, c'est parce qu'ils ont une disposition intérieure toute sainte et que ce qu'ils entendent dire de notre religion y est conforme. Ils sentent qu'un Dieu les a faits. Il ne veulent aimer que Dieu, ils ne veulent haïr qu'eux-mêmes. (Fr. 381)

It is not, of course, to these that Pascal addresses himself; nor does their kind of belief correspond exactly to the end he has in view, though that *disposition intérieure* is part of his objective. As an apologist, as a persuader concerning matters of faith, he speaks to the one who will believe some day, he hopes, but that person or seeker will have not only the inner grace. He will have an intellectual preparation and armature as well. He will have reasoned out by proofs and by exegesis of the Bible whatever can be reasoned out. Third, those who do not search, who spend their time in diversions, are the primary targets, and Pascal wants to stir them to the point of joining the class of seekers. He knows that he will not succeed in every instance. The effort will not be completely vain, however, for those left behind bear witness in their stubborn and unwitting way to the whole truth being pursued by the real searchers.

The Seeker's Path

Pascal's seeker sets out on the long path that leads to readiness. After some skirmishes with his mentor he begins to understand his own experience and to interpret his observations of others—of various types of people, some hoisting themselves by their own bootstraps or trying to do so, some giving themselves unthinkingly to pastimes, some becoming more and more aware of intermittences in their own lives and of oscillations between values and pleasures with no end in sight.[1] From this degree of insight he may go on to consult the specialists in knowing and doing, the philosophers, only to find that the fundamental problem repeats itself in an atmosphere of sectarian pride and further contradictions. Each of the two schools of philosophers, the Stoics-dogmatists and the Epicureans-skeptics, sees and promotes by turns an important side of the truth but misses the fact that their oppositions and controversies are complementary. And so their solutions are invalid: they have not discovered that the problem calls for reconciliation on a higher level than that of mere self-assertion. Then the searcher arrives onto the plane of religion and the religious interpretation of experience. Here Pascal calls upon him to look before and after. He must look before in an effort to discern how and why he came to his present state, and after in an attempt to answer questions about the future, which just may open onto eternity.

On this plane of religious insight the seeker finds himself once again in the presence of a multiplicity about which he must do something (earlier it consisted in the refutations that the philosophers direct to each other). For there are a number of religions: pagan, Islamic, and Chinese, among others. His problem will no longer be struggling with a dilemma; it becomes a matter of discrimination rather than of harmonizing contraries. (Pascal is not about to allow substantial truth to a religion other than the Christian!) The character of the problem gives this part of the argument a particular turn. With the help of the apologist, the seeker draws up a list of the *marques de vérité*, and, using this standard, he may test conflicting traditions and doctrines. Before long—at least this is the dénouement provided by Pascal—he sees on the basis of evidence like the prophecies, proofs, and miracles contained in the Bible or associated with the religion of which it is the center, that there is a doctrine so conceived and elaborated that it can return to the original paradox—the simultaneous greatness and baseness of man—and disclose in it the integral truth about human nature in its fallen state. Furthermore, after the explanation based on original sin, this same doctrine goes on to show how a two-pronged initiative of God, rooted in his justice and mercy, redeems our two vicious tendencies to pride and concupiscence (actually two sides of the same thing: self-love). This doctrine alone, Pascal believes, goes beyond the limits of common and philosophical experience. It alone furnishes both a diagnosis and a remedy for the human predicament in satisfactory terms, which are properly *religious*.

The seeker may end his study of religions and of Scripture, with its allegedly decisive prophecies and realizations, in an unconvinced frame of mind. Pascal himself admits that his collection of proofs is not truly conclusive; and he is quite capable of using our hopes and fears and especially the fear of death as a means of persuasion. In this part of his case Pascal places the accent definitely on what comes after rather than before the present and this life. His seeker is forced to agree that the disproportion between God as infinite being and us as finite beings is too great for us ever to reach the certainty that God exists (to say nothing of knowing His nature) by the natural light of reason. But he may take some comfort in a probability, which has a positive value, even though it does not compel as a demonstration compels. Alongside the arguments drawn from biblical exegesis he can put considerations that, in their most specific form, are expressed in the calculated terms of the wager. The things he will have to give up or bet are little or nothing in comparison to the possible gains. Pascal assures him that after he has tried for a while thinking and living by the *as ifs* of the next stage of his evolution, the seeker will realize that he has given up nothing and gained everything. He has in fact bet on a certainty.

As I have presented the whole apologetic argument, treating it as a matter of retrospective and prospective views, the wager has come in second place. But in fragment 418 itself Pascal thinks first of the wager and then of taking up the Bible to get from it light on the concealed part ("le dessous") of the game. One gets a quick "demonstration" to the effect that behaving as though God exists is not repugnant to reason—far from it—and then one may fill out the details by going to the Bible. The exact order followed here seems to me to be relatively unimportant; what is essential is that Pascal has engaged in all this proving activity for the benefit of the mind, of reason. The second of our *deux pièces*, which is heart, or even more than that, our total self apart from worked-out, discursive thinking is the last obstacle to be surmounted. It must be approached in terms of habituation and custom, as we have seen in the preceding chapter. By repeatedly acting as if the *morale chrétienne* were true, the seeker finds that his passions are quieted. He loosens gradually the bonds that concupiscence has formed between him and things. And, of course, he finds that his belief, motivated originally by inductive and mathematical proofs, is becoming stronger, since cus-

tom affects the mind as well as the heart. He senses that
the final experience is near, and that his heart is being
polarized, in readiness for an event involving himself and
the hidden God: *Dieu sensible au cœur, non à la raison*.

The Heart as Recipient and Faculty

As with any important item in Pascal's vocabulary, we find
it helpful to review his way of using the word "cœur." I see
three typical usages: literal, idiomatic, and figurative. (1)
Actually there seems to be only one instance of "cœur"
where it refers to the physical organ. Fragment 65 begins
with a title word, "Diversité," and then continues:

> La théologie est une science, mais en même temps
> combien est-ce de sciences? Un homme est un suppôt,
> mais si on l'anatomise que sera-ce? la tête, le [*var.* bras]
> cœur, l'estomac, les veines, chaque veine, chaque por-
> tion de veine, le sang, chaque humeur de sang.

Even here "cœur" appears in what would have been an
analogy if it had been fully worked out, and the principal
term of the comparison would have been theology rather
than man. The passage starts us also along one of those
infinite series tending in the direction of the infinitely
small; it reminds us of Pascal's variation on this theme
apropos of the *ciron*. One may fairly conclude that the heart
as a physical organ does not interest Pascal very much. (2)
In the second place we find it in locutions like "de bon
cœur," "de tout son cœur," and "manquer de cœur."
Already these phrases take us into the moral domain and
the figurative use of the word. (3) As we study the uses of
"cœur" as a moral factor in the personality or, to use language closer to that of Pascal, in the soul, we are struck by
the fact that the heart seems at times less a part in a whole
than a whole in a whole. After all, it exercises two characteristic functions of the soul: it knows and it desires, and

thus can have the role of a quasi-human agent within the human agent. In a way it has foreign or external relations with the rest of our being and especially with the mind ("esprit").

If we turn from that first general impression to the heart as Pascal imagines and conceives it in detail, we must note in his habit of language two main lines of association and thought. There is the image of the container and the contained, with the accompanying concern about what is in the heart and who put it there. The second way of thinking is based on the image or notion of a power and its movement toward action and objects. Fragment 139 gives us, in a classic concluding line, a good example of the first kind of thought and imagery. Pascal says that from childhood people burden us with concerns about honor, fortune, health—our own and that of our friends. It is a strange way to make us happy (that being the presumed end). Then, lest we think that our goal should be to free ourselves from such obligations, he administers the second shock: if the burdens were all removed, we would indeed be unhappy, since it is only because of those distractions that we have the possibility of not seeing ourselves and of not knowing our miserable state. Then comes the conclusion: "Que le cœur de l'homme est creux et plein d'ordure." Another good example in this vein occurs in fragment 136:

> Car ou l'on pense aux misères qu'on a ou à celles qui nous menacent. Et quand on se verrait même assez à l'abri de toutes parts l'ennui de son autorité privée ne laisserait pas de sortir du fond du cœur où il a des racines naturelles, et de remplir l'esprit de son venin.

Other passages mention specific contents to be found in the heart, such as *malignité* or original sin (fr. 278), unfeelingness (fr. 427), preoccupation with renown (fr. 470). Fragment 627 speaks of vanity "anchored in the heart." In fragment 485 there is a sentence where Pascal uses the verb "s'enfler" with the heart as its subject: it "swells." To a certain point the picture is dark, unpromising and negative when one looks into the heart. But that is only one side of Pascal's view. Qualities found in the heart come from man and creatures or they come from God; so far we have considered only the former. In many texts scattered through the *Pensées* the colors in the picture change, according to the swing of the argument. On the positive side Pascal sees in the heart, as a result of God's action, the fear of God (fr. 346), the presence of the law (fr. 346); or again, in an order of ideas that suggests the New Testament, spirit (fr. 328), grace (fr. 172), and faith (fr. 7), and reason (fr. 172); or, once more, states of consolation, love, and joy (fr. 449). In the bottom of one's heart, beneath the appearances and subterfuges, one finds either God or his creatures and an inclination to love the one more than the other.

This leads us to the second line of thought and imagery concerning the heart: that of a power, a tendency directed toward one or another object known or pursued as its end. Dynamism and movement characterize this way of imagining and conceiving the heart. Here the best way to proceed is no doubt to start at the end of a line and work backward, remembering always the basic opposition between negative and positive impulses, and also the joint activity of knowing and loving.[2] At each step in the analysis, some specification of these aspects of the situation or of the data pertinent to them will occur. Of course the degree of elaboration varies greatly from fragment to fragment, and at times one can only go on by way of inference.

1. Beginning then with the *object* or *objects* toward which the heart orients itself, we find God, as "sensible au cœur" (fr. 424), which suggests the action of the heart in knowing, and we find the affirmation of a natural love for a universal being, which suggests the other register, that of

loving. But we also meet at this stage an opposing love, centered on creatures, and especially on the self. It is the characteristic theme of *le moi haïssable*. In fact, these two terms are closely related: love of God implies hatred of self, and love of self implies hatred of God.

2. Behind the objects known or sought lies the *operation* of the heart. Several fragments give some insight into the precise way Pascal thought of this point along our line. In fragment 110 the heart knows and knows intuitively ideas like number, space, time, movement, and supplies them to the reason for use in its demonstrations, and it sees spontaneously, against the opinions or arguments of the Pyrrhonians, that life is not a dream, that there is a difference between sleeping and waking. We must mention here also—in the sphere of operation as love and pursuit—a number of instances where Pascal uses the idiomatic expression "de tout son cœur" to modify the verbs "aimer" and "chercher": there we have in simplest form and also in the strongest form a statement of what the heart does, and how it does it: either wholeheartedly or halfheartedly (as in fr. 149). The adverbs supply at this stage the positive or negative shading. For the obvious example, one should always love God in the former way, *de tout son cœur*.

3. Behind the operations of the heart lie its acquired *dispositions* to act in love or knowledge. Habits involving the passions are an excellent example of the problem at this point. They coincide actually with the habits of *divertissement*. The search for diversion, for some particular good taken as the object (even though one may know in lucid moments that it will never satisfy and that possessing it is not the answer) becomes a more or less steady inclination. There is no need to cite fragments based on this fundamental theme. The remedy here consists in changing effectively the direction of one's loves, a reversal that is possible if one adopts on a trial basis a line of action or behavior that assumes the rightness of Christian morality. The penitence

it may bring leads to absolution on the part of God (as in fr. 923: "Dieu absout aussitôt qu'il voit la pénitence dans le cœur"). In Old Testament language and citations, this change of heart is described in terms of figurative *circoncision*. This process of purification, whereby the soul is rendered capable of God, corresponds perfectly to the new moral direction defined in those fragments where the attention centers not so much on the Bible and on exegesis as on the reader-seeker whom the apologist is trying to persuade. As a counterpart of this effort comes a gesture on the part of God: He is described as inclining hearts (fr. 382), as revealing Himself to those whose hearts have been cleared of their evil dispositions.

4. A problem more serious than rehabilitation faces us now in the soul. For underneath the perverse bents lies a complex state, *ennui*. In one sense one may describe it as an emptiness, a dynamic emptiness. Fragment 622, which has as its title the word "Ennui," defines the term in all its terrible force.

> Rien n'est si insupportable à l'homme que d'être dans un plein repos, sans affaires, sans divertissement, sans application.
> Il sent alors son néant, son abandon, son insuffisance, sa dépendance, son impuissance, son vide.
> Incontinent il sortira du fond de son âme l'ennui, la noirceur, la tristesse, le chagrin, le dépit, le désespoir.

This psychic state, arising from an act of introspection and intuition, gives a desperate awareness of what one is like when all the other layers have been removed. I call it dynamic because it has one important consequence: it impels us to seek relief in distractions and pastimes. The sight of the *fond de l'âme* is too much to bear. The trouble is, though, that we come to understand the significance of distractions and the anesthetic function they have. That realization undermines their effectiveness, and we are back where we began. But this emptiness, when taken as a moral principle, can be further specified. Actually at the bottom of the heart lies an innate *malignité*, which inclines us to put self in the center of everything, to go for the lower instead of the higher value and for the material instead of the spiritual. Indulging in *divertissements* implies a mistaking of proper ends and objects; the malignity now in question is more profound, because there is really no mistake, just perverse impulse. Obviously we are talking about original sin and its result. The present state of man, underneath all possible physical and mental additions, is a fallen one. Pascal's analysis of man's condition is intended to show the vivid reality of the flaw in human nature, and his interpretation of the Scriptures proves, he thinks, that the flaw was present from the beginning of history, along with veiled promises of deliverance from it. The biblical account reinforces the glimmer that every man has of having known innocence. For how could he have a sense of his imperfect and degraded state, except by some obscure memory of life before the appearance of evil in him and his world?

5. Thus we arrive at the original and deepest level of the heart. In its Edenic existence, it had no effective distractions; it was pure tendency toward Truth and Good; and it had the good fortune of being direct communication with a supreme object, the Object for which in fact the tendency was created in the first place.

To Conclude on the Side of the Seeker

It is now time to pick up once more the thread of the discussion. Clearly, when the seeker's mind is properly disposed, and his heart likewise, and when custom has done its work, he is ready for a culminating experience of which the heart is to be the theater.[3] There the search for a certain faith will end. But I have thought that of all the

complex realities involved in this progression—mind, custom, and heart—the last required detailed treatment. What
seemed, perhaps, a digression has brought us to the center
of the mysterious event that interests us most; it lessens
the risk of our conceiving that process in a remote, superfi-
cial, or mechanical way. It is only after we know what is in
the heart, according to Pascal, and how it got there that we
shall have a chance to grasp in adequate—if one may use
such a word at this point—and characteristic terms the
final moment, as Pascal sheds what light he can on the
meeting of man and God. And, a fortiori, we must know as
much as we can about the vital energies of the heart in
knowing, loving, and seeking, if we are to understand
what takes place in that encounter.

God: First Distinctions

God is the other agent in the drama of assent and certainty.
On His part, just as much as on the side of the seeker, it is
true to say that what happens at the last moment has its
proper meaning and force when seen against a complicated background. For the seeker the leading idea is that of
a search for something that will satisfy fully a paradoxical
creature; and on the other side, the leading idea would
seem to be that of a gift, tendered by a Giver who is also
paradoxical, for He is both hidden and accessible, concealed and revealed. But many other elements are directly
or indirectly relevant to the experience of a certain faith.

If we are to begin at the beginning, it is premature to
speak of a giver and his gift. With what prior ideas and
distinctions does Pascal work? (1) There is the *Dieu des
philosophes*, who awakens two trains of thought in Pascal's
mind. The *deists* demonstrate the existence of God, on the
basis of what they see in the nature and motions of creatures. Pascal dismisses them always peremptorily, saying
either that they can only be convincing to those who al-

ready believe, or that their demonstrations are too technical and can have no lasting effect. One becomes doubtful
soon after hearing such reasoning: it may have been incomplete or wrong or misunderstood. The *Stoics* have an
elevated conception of God as Providence, as one whose
will is in the order of things; and they see the wisdom
of man as consisting in conformity to that will. It is a
high ideal and one that is correctly oriented, but Pascal
dismisses it also, because man is expected to realize it
essentially through self-mastery, with some help from
philosopher-teachers like Epictetus. The task is impossible
and the effort doomed to frustration, because human limits
are not recognized in this view, nor does it perceive the
consequent need for other than human help. (2) There are
the gods of other religions. Pascal is quite aware of the fact
that he is treating two distinct problems, that of belief and
how one reaches it, and that of conflicting or contradictory
objects of belief. As he invites us to go beyond the level of
philosophical thinking about God and up to the level of
religion, he knows that he must face with us the disturbing
fact of different and competing gods—in Egypt, in Greece
and Rome, in Islam, in China. One by one or collectively,
depending on what is uppermost in his mind, he eliminates them by reference to something like a table of *marques
de vérité*: they lack one or more decisive traits such as scriptural revelation, *perpétuité*, prophecies (I mean *accomplished*
prophecies, such as those in the Judeo-Christian religion),
miracles, witnesses, and full knowledge of man's *contrariétés* and needs.[4]

God and History

That leaves, of course, the religion that does have the
marks of truth, all of them, and the God of Abraham,
Isaac, and Jacob. First and foremost, it would seem, he is a
God who intervenes in history and has done so from the

very beginning—especially in the history of man.[5] Pascal sees an unbroken sequence from the creation down into the seventeenth century (and destined to continue to the end of time). There was a people with a law, a book, and prophets. The Redeemer awaited from the time of man's fall did come as prophesied, and the Church began under divine auspices with the coming of the Holy Spirit. The pagan world was converted; and since then the Church, the sign and teacher of a new relationship between God and man, has moved without break down the centuries. In the combats between Jesuits and Jansenists the God of that Church is working; and He still performs miracles, as Pascal knew from the incident of the cure effected by the *Sainte-Epine*.

In this great sequence of events—not yet completed—Pascal sees something true at every stage and in every time. The key to history in this account is the problem of man's destiny, and how one defines that problem. Really to solve it necessitates assenting to two great truths: that man is corrupt by nature, incapable of realizing what he wants (*vouloir et ne pouvoir*: that is his predicament in attempting to know the truth and to achieve happiness), and that there is a religious answer. In the procession of history God is revealing—not totally and tyrannically, but partially, often by signs and nonviolently—what the destiny of man properly is and can be. Another way of saying this is to point to the doctrine that emerges from the Bible and the tradition of the Church. And that leads to Pascal's next step: a consideration of the *morale* that follows from the doctrine, for actions are implied and dictated by the doctrine. There is a sense in which every man is involved in this vast enterprise, and in the problem that lies at its center. Every man situates himself by acts if not by conscious choice with reference to an unavoidable alternative. The key to history gives the key to personal life—*sans Dieu ou avec Dieu*.

God and Prophets

Not only does God intervene in human lives on the massive scale of history but also in the existences of particular people. Pascal shifts easily from one viewpoint to the other, from God-and-man to God-and-men. Some of the most obvious examples of this kind of inspiration are furnished by the prophets. In one sense their prophecies represent instances in which God has chosen to speak of Himself. That is, perhaps, what Pascal was referring to when he wrote in fragment 303 of artisans who talk of wealth, of lawyers who talk of war and royalty, the implication being that they are out of their element and necessarily speak badly of such subjects, whereas:

> . . . le riche parle bien des richesses, le roi parle froidement d'un grand don qu'il vient de faire, et Dieu parle bien de Dieu.

However, from the point of view of the subject, of the man through whom God speaks, what happens in prophesy results from something almost exactly like the experience of conversion. Or, more precisely, what happens there presupposes conversion, and the familiar vocabulary appears in both instances.

> Qu'alors on n'enseignera plus son prochain disant: voici le Seigneur. Car Dieu se fera [*var.* connaître] sentir à tous. Vos fils prophétiseront. Je mettrai mon esprit et ma crainte en votre cœur.
> Tout cela est la même chose.
> Prophétiser c'est parler de Dieu, non par preuves de dehors, mais par sentiment intérieur et immédiat. (Fr. 328)

This curious passage reveals two interesting things. In the first place we see how Pascal starts with the Bible, putting texts together from two prophets—mainly from Jeremiah 30:33–34, but also from Joel 2:28—through the end of the first paragraph. Then his commentary and his conclusion follow; and there his personal vocabulary begins to take over. (The variant already contains an indication of this shift: he prefers the verb "sentir" to "connaître" in the matter of knowing God.) In the next place we see how he understands prophecy and its relation to conversion. It consists of speech based not on proofs, but on the immediate, underived, felt conviction that Pascal regularly assigns to inspiration and the end of the search. We are not far from the familiar antithesis between *esprit* and *cœur* and their respective ways of proceeding, the former by reasons and the latter by *sentiment*.

One is tempted to think that Pascal saw in himself the presence of the prophetic nature and disposition. In his *Pensées* and in the apologetic portion or project (I have in mind the less "demonstrative" pages or fragments) he speaks from the heart and according to its order, and he had received once at least something like the outpouring of the Spirit mentioned in his quotations from the Bible. It is also interesting to note that when he made up his pseudonyms, two of them include biblical names. One belonged to a divinely-inspired king and the other to a prophet: *Salomon* de Tultie and *Amos* Dettonville.

Be that as it may, the kind of mass conversion described in the text from Jeremiah—"they will all know me, the least no less than the greatest"—and conceived as a source of prophecy introduces us to essential aspects or qualities of the climactic experience to be studied here as the last of the means of belief. It is internal, immediate, centered in the heart, and initiated by God.

The Seeker Finds

Pascal treats the divine initiative in various ways, as is clear from some salient verbs. Each has particular force and resonance because of its etymology and biblical connotations. "Incliner," as in fragment 380 and a number of others, suggests a turn, a push, a disposition: God inclines the heart; "inspirer," as in fragment 382 and others, suggests in-breathing, a reception of the Spirit; "éclaircir" and "éclairer," as in fragments 252, 236, 513 and 835, suggest the coming of light and sight, as opposed to darkness, obscurity, and blindness; "se découvrir," as in fragments 438, 444, and 793, evokes images of uncovering, of self-revelation.

There is no denying that we do glimpse the nature of God's activity through these verbs, of which He is often the subject, but of course we must add to these valuable clues much other and, in a sense, richer evidence concerning the heart, the objects that determine events within its recesses, and the kind of certainty attained at last by the seeker. In the context of prophecy, where an outpouring of the Spirit is received in the heart of the prophet and expressed in words that belong only accidentally to him (since it is God who speaks via the prophet), Pascal tends to fall back on the imagery of container/contained and of vehicle/message. In other discussions that bear more closely on our present concern, which is the experience of certainty, he thinks in a more elaborate and less peremptory way and uses his doctrine of powers, acts, and objects. As his language shows, any attempt to imagine how the outpouring of the Spirit or the filling by the Spirit occurs evokes the image of a God outside us and acting upon us from without, but when Pascal thinks in terms of powers and their operations, God comes closer, he joins himself to us. Even this phrasing will not bear much scrutiny, for no matter how we go about our exposition, we must make what sense we can of this crucial statement in fragment 407: "Le bonheur n'est ni hors de nous ni dans nous; il est en Dieu et hors nous et dans nous." Pascal himself had some trouble here. According to the variant he apparently first thought of writing: "il est en Dieu ni hors

ni dans nous." My main point is that there are a number of
texts that show us another way of analyzing the experience
of inspiration and lead us away from the strongly
metaphorical biblical language to a more literal vocabulary,
one that permits us to discern aspects, motions, changes.
The result is a subtler, more satisfactory picture than we
might otherwise have—provided always that we avoid
making Pascal's distinctions more rigid than they really
are. What counts above all is their capacity to support each
other, to fuse, and to take on life.

Although the general direction of the argument is from
the outside in, from the outer to the inner man, Pascal does
not disqualify external behavior.

> Il faut que l'extérieur soit joint à l'intérieur pour ob-
> tenir de Dieu; c'est-à-dire que l'on se mette à genoux,
> prie des lèvres, etc. afin que l'homme qui n'a voulu se
> soumettre à Dieu soit maintenant soumis à la créature.
> Attendre de cet extérieur le secours est être [*var*. idolâ-
> tre] superstitieux; ne vouloir pas le joindre à l'intérieur
> est être superbe. (Fr. 944)

The thought of this fragment recalls strikingly that of the
wager and the "cela vous abêtira." It also refers, I think, by
an association that is not far fetched, to our dual composition (*automate, esprit*), and especially to the automatic side,
which is ruled by custom. Once within the psyche Pascal
turns—in the search for inspiration—away from mind
("esprit") and reasoning. Again and again in the *Pensées* he
insists on the theme expressed in fragment 424 as "Dieu
sensible au cœur, non à la raison"; we have already seen
above the short but very significant sentence, "Dieu se fera
sentir à tous" (fr. 328); and of course this transaction will
result in an affective experience, a "sentiment de cœur"
(fr. 110). The vocabulary of feeling is consistent and om-
nipresent. In all these references the seat is obviously the
heart; and after it has been prepared and purified, it is the

place where God will reveal Himself in a gift. The insistence on something other than reason and reasoning is summed up in fragment 588:

> La foi est un don de Dieu. Ne croyez pas que nous disions que c'est un don de raisonnement. Les autres religions ne disent pas cela de leur foi. Elles ne donnaient que le raisonnement pour y arriver, qui n'y mène pas néanmoins.

Faith understood as a gift, and a gift not of reason, is a mark that sets the Christian religion apart.

In giving up reason at this point, however, we do not give up knowing. We meet here once more the fundamental ambiguity of the heart, as a place of knowing as well as of feeling and loving. It would be a mistake to shut off from each other these two aspects of the heart's activity, though we may usefully distinguish them, and show how they imply each other. In the heart love is not blind, nor is knowledge without warmth. The cooperation, the fusion even, of these two functions is something always to remember in reading the *Pensées*. To that ambiguity another must be added. It is best grasped, perhaps, as a contrast of orientations, based on differences in the objects known and loved. (1) Keeping in mind the intimate connections of knowing and loving (or desiring), we note that in one phase the heart knows finite things and their principles of intelligibility, and it loves either itself primarily or other creatures with reference to itself. (2) Or, again, it is led onto a new terrain, where it knows an infinite being and awakens to the fact that it loves God rather than itself. How the heightening of the knowing faculty occurs—to Pascal it requires the overcoming of a "disproportion"—we shall inquire into later.

When the inner revolution begins, and after it has made some headway, it is as though the seeker looks backward. A strongly worded antithesis appears. Here it is expressed in a fragment that deals with uncomplicated people, rather than with those whose itinerary has been long before reaching this point:

> Ne vous étonnez pas de voir des personnes simples croire sans raisonnement. Dieu leur donne l'amour de soi et la haine d'eux-mêmes. Il incline leur cœur à croire. One ne croira jamais, d'une créance utile et de foi si Dieu n'incline le cœur et on croira dès qu'il l'inclinera.
>
> Et c'est ce que David connaissait bien. *Inclina cor meum deus in* etc. (Fr. 380)

I cite the whole fragment because of the extreme concision with which so much of what we have been discussing is said. Of course the antithesis to notice is the love of God and the hatred of self that coexist in the hearts of the "personnes simples," and also in that of the persistent seeker, when he has come to this stage. Another fragment (373) says it in one forceful line: "Il faut n'aimer que Dieu et ne haïr que soi." What makes this situation so tense is that the God in question is a judge, one who is aware of all the flaws and secrets, who evaluates actions and is capable of wrath—in fact, He is entitled to it. We are thrown back into horror at our concupiscence, that innate tendency to error and vice. And yet, there is in us still a spark of the right love, for as Pascal tells us in fragment 444, " . . . les hommes sont tout ensemble indignes de Dieu et capables de Dieu: indignes par leur corruption, capables par leur première nature." It is a variation on the *misère* and *grandeur* theme. But we have gone far beyond the confused exchanges of the philosophers; greatness is not indicated by the power of thought, nor even in the perception of one's wretchedness, which serves at one stage of the argument as a title to dignity; the positive quality left is a capacity only, something not yet realized. Having traveled the way of intellectual and moral preparation and nearing the moment of knowing God effectively in faith, the seeker and we, if we have chosen to follow him, find ourselves stripped to the core, transparent to the divine eye, and near annihilation.

The terrible tension, the distance between man and God, the sense of seeing but also of being seen (and judged): these are never removed in the rest of Pascal's analysis. What happens is that he adds a third and mediating term and thus makes communication possible. Sometimes, as his mind and imagination range over the triad of God, Jesus Christ, and man, he dwells on the original break and how it came about. Looking back to passages in the Old Testament, he paints a picture (in fragment 456) of the philosophical sects coming into being and then ceasing to be, while in one corner of the world some people are declaring that everyone is in error, that God has revealed the truth to them.

> En effet, toutes les autres sectes cessent; celle-là dure toujours et depuis 4.000 ans ils déclarent qu'ils tiennent de leurs ancêtres que l'homme est déchu de la communication avec Dieu dans un entier éloignement de Dieu, mais qu'il a promis de les racheter . . .

Or, again, in fragment 205, starting from a slightly different angle—our inability to love something other than ourselves not to mention something unknown to us—he shows religion instructing us in our duties and in what we need to know.

> Elle [la religion] nous apprend que par un homme tout a été perdu et la liaison rompue entre Dieu et nous, et que par un homme la liaison est réparée.

Or, once more, in fragment 781, starting from the pretensions of the deists, who think their demonstrations of God by the works of Nature will help those who lack faith, Pascal says that Scripture knows better than they and speaks better of God.

> Ce n'est pas de cette sorte que l'Ecriture qui connaît mieux les choses qui sont de Dieu en parle. Elle dit au

contraire que Dieu est un Dieu caché et que depuis la
corruption de la nature il les a laissés dans un aveugle-
ment dont ils ne peuvent sortir que par J.-C. hors duquel
toute communication avec Dieu est ôtée. *Nemo novit pa-
trem nisi filius et cui filius voluit revelare.*

Jesus Christ is, then, the mediator and the only mediator,
the only link that can restore the communication between
God and man.

Pascal emphasizes this exclusive claim in still another
passage (fr. 291), where the contrast is in effect drawn
between facts within the Christian religion, rather than
between deism and Scripture.

Cette religion si grande en miracles, saints, purs, ir-
réprochables, savants et grands témoins, martyrs;
rois—David—établis; Isaïe prince du sang; si grande en
science après avoir étalé tous ses miracles et toute sa
sagesse, elle réprouve tout cela et dit qu'elle n'a ni
sagesse, ni signe, mais la croix et la folie.

The religion that by signs and wisdom has established its
authority and credibility turns its back on all that, declaring
that we must look elsewhere if we would change and become in fact capable of communication with God. The
paradoxical fact of mediation by this mysterious means is
clarified somewhat if we note that Christ is not just the
counterpart of Adam, not simply the bearer of a wisdom
that is a folly. In fragment 449 Pascal analyzes a situation in
which unnamed and misguided disputants try to refute
Christianity on the ground that it consists merely in the
adoration of a great, powerful, and eternal God. In fact
they are refuting the God of deism, which is almost as far
from Christianity as atheism pure and simple.

Mais qu'ils en concluent ce qu'ils voudront contre le
déisme, ils n'en concluront rien contre la religion
chrétienne, qui consiste proprement au mystère du Rédempteur, qui unissant en lui les deux natures, humaine

et divine, a retiré les hommes de la corruption du péché pour les réconcilier à Dieu en sa personne divine.

A return to the point of view of the human subject gives us more details about the person and role of the mediator. As knowers—if we accept Pascal's premises—we depend on Christ as a principle of understanding.

Non seulement nous ne connaissons Dieu que par Jésus-Christ mais nous ne nous connaissons nous-mêmes que par J.-C.; nous ne connaissons la vie, la mort que par Jésus-Christ. Hors de J.-C. nous ne savons ce que c'est ni que notre vie ni que notre mort, ni que Dieu, ni que nous-mêmes. (Fr. 417)

Pascal follows this with an affirmation of the importance of Scripture. Without Jesus Christ we know nothing, but we would not know of him were it not for the Bible, of which he is the central figure ("l'Ecriture qui n'a que lui pour objet"). Here and there, in the analysis of what we know of God and of ourselves thanks to this mediator, we redis-cover the theme of *grandeur* and *misère* as it is rooted in common experience and then relived and rethought by the philosophers. Here is fragment 192 in its entirety:

La connaissance de Dieu sans celle de sa misère fait l'orgueil.
La connaissance de sa misère sans celle de Dieu fait le désespoir.
La connaissance de J.-C. [*var.* forme] fait le milieu parce que nous y trouvons, et Dieu et notre misère.

The main terms of this formulation are reproduced in fragment 449, along with an explicit allusion to the *philosophes*.

...il est également dangereux à l'homme de connaître Dieu sans connaître sa misère et de connaître sa misère sans connaître le Rédempteur qui l'en peut guérir. Une seule de ces connaissances fait, ou la superbe des philosophes, qui ont connu Dieu et non leur misère, ou le désespoir des athées, qui connaissent leur misère sans Rédempteur.

The reference to the pride of the philosophers seems addressed to the Stoics and dogmatists. As for the *athées*, I believe it would not be incorrect to link them with the Pyrrhonians who merge into the Epicureans, or vice versa, depending on whether one stresses knowledge or behavior. In any case, whether we are talking of the experience of men or the ideas and attitudes of philosophers, it is important that man, the subject-term in the triad, see his place, locate himself with regard to Jesus Christ and to God. Two propositions—they were implied in phrases like "connaître sa misère" and "connaître Dieu"—emerge in clear and parallel form; on these two truths hangs all the rest of the argument:

(1) "qu'il y a un Dieu: dont les hommes sont capables";
(2) "qu'il y a une corruption dans la nature, qui les en rend indignes."

Man must know these two points; and by the mercy of God through the Scripture he can know them. These are, as we see in fragment 449, the two *chefs* of the Christian religion.

Qu'on examine l'ordre du monde sur cela et qu'on voie si toutes choses ne tendent pas à l'établissement des deux chefs de cette religion: Jésus-Christ est l'objet de tout, le centre où tout tend. Qui le connaît connaît la raison de toutes choses.

Dieu et notre misère: that is what we must know, and one without the other is fatal.

This brings us back to the earlier phase of this discussion, to the basic intuition of the believer as hatred of self and love of God. That was the negative phase of the argument, the phase of opposition without resolution. It is already a step forward, since it goes beyond the sort of tension expressed in formulas like *misère et grandeur de l'homme*. There the greatness in question was separated from the notion of God; it was the privilege or dignity of thought that Pascal was setting against the pettinesses and distractions and pleasures of man. At this later point in the evolution of the seeker the function of the term "grandeur" has been taken over by God. The new antithesis brings not puzzlement, such as one experiences in the *renversement continuel*, but a stable tension between God and self. That two-term formulation is still not the final stage of the argument as we have just seen: it prepares the way for Jesus Christ. Pascal develops important contradictions so that he may reconcile and unify them. Hence the provision of a third stage, and the triadic way of stating how the heart knows and loves in the critical moment of conversion. Again and again that is the way Pascalian dialectic works: he locates a subject in which a contradiction inheres, and after suitable amplification of that paradox, he posits a comprehensive or mediating term toward which the opposed impulses, ideas, or things may be oriented.

All the essential data of the experience we are defining appear in fragment 378. The subject is, precisely, conversion. Pascal imagines a group made up of people who say glibly, "If I had seen a miracle, I would convert" ("je me convertirais"). How can they be sure of doing something they do not really understand? They have only *their* idea of what conversion is—"un commerce et une conversation telle qu'ils se la figurent." Pascal sets aside this wrong conception without further comment, but he is quite unequivocal about the right one.

> La conversion véritable consiste à s'anéantir devant cet être universel qu'on a irrité tant de fois et qui vous peut perdre légitimement à toute heure, à reconnaître qu'on ne peut rien sans lui et qu'on n'a rien mérité de lui que sa disgrâce. Elle consiste à connaître qu'*il y a une*

opposition invincible entre Dieu et nous et que sans un média-
teur il ne peut y avoir de commerce. (Fr. 378; italics added)

There are in fact two ways of looking at conversion, and
Pascal has it both ways. He analyzes it, in terms of contraries and resolutions, but he also describes it. The two
phases of dialectic give way to the experience itself, to the
moral and religious event as distinct from the analytical
view of its contents. The language and imagery of inspiration reappear.

> Mais le Dieu d'Abraham, le Dieu d'Isaac, le Dieu de
> Jacob, le Dieu des chrétiens est un Dieu d'amour et
> de consolation; c'est un Dieu qui remplit l'âme et le
> cœur de ceux qu'il possède; c'est un Dieu qui leur fait
> sentir intérieurement leur misère et sa miséricorde
> infinie; qui s'unit au fond de leur âme; qui la remplit
> d'humilité, de joie, de confiance, d'amour; qui les rend
> incapables d'autre fin que de lui-même. (Fr. 449)

Proportions and the Narrowing of the Gap

Now conversion is, in part, an act of knowing, and Pascal
has, if not a theory of knowing, at least some definite ideas
about how it takes place. They take us beyond the logical
devices just analyzed and the indications—biblical rather
than logical in origin—of inspiration, feeling, saturation,
longing. His *idée de derrière* in the area of knowing seems to
be drawn from geometry, although the principle involved
is not necessarily mathematical: I mean the conception of
proportion. The fundamental proposition runs like this. In
order for knowledge to occur, there must be a proportion
between the knower and the known. At the outset of any
act of knowing, we must have a correspondence of essential aspects between the knower and the object to which he
turns his attention; and what happens thereafter is a kind
of adjustment or specification of the knower to the

known.[6] Here is a curiously indirect example of the principle at work:

> Les villes par où on passe on ne se soucie pas d'y être estimé. Mais quand on y doit demeurer un peu de temps on s'en soucie. Combien de temps faut-il? Un temps proportionné à notre durée chétive. (Fr. 31)

Of course Pascal presents more elaborate and abstract statements of his views on these noetic proportions; and, characteristically, he explores with particular intensity the problem of *disproportion* between knower and known, and works out the consequences of such anomaly.

Indeed, it is by examining the concept of disproportion, as it appears in fragment 199 for example, that we can form the most accurate idea of his "epistemology." That famous fragment takes knowers and what they want to know and engages them in a tissue of disproportions, plainly exhibited, that are humbling, that put man in his place (which turns out to be indefinable!). Pascal does two things in this text: (1) he indicates the disproportions, and (2) he draws moral consequences from them. Here it is the former that interest us particularly. Quantitatively speaking, in terms of size or *masse*, nature stretches in two directions, toward infinites of largeness and smallness; and man is finite. What can he make of nature? What can he hope to know of it? To Pascal it is obvious, since knowledge requires proportion as a *sine qua non*, that the finite creature will never grasp the beginning and end of things: because of their intrinsic limits, his imagination and mind cannot attain that which is unlimited. So much for the ambitious scientists of his day. At the next change of the reasoning, Pascal declares us to be unable even to know the middle range of being, our customary and ordinary milieu, because to know the parts we must know the whole—and that forever eludes us. Hence the disproportion between the *finite* and the *finite*! In a fine display of logical and rhetorical virtuosity, Pascal goes on to show that as combinations of matter and mind we are by nature out of proportion to either matter or mind as it is in itself, and can therefore understand neither; and he ends this *morceau de bravoure* by reminding us that the most incomprehensible thing of all is the union of the two substances.

> C'est néanmoins la chose qu'on comprend le moins; l'homme est à lui-même le plus prodigieux objet de la nature, car il ne peut concevoir ni ce que c'est que corps, et encore moins ce que c'est qu'esprit, et moins qu'aucune chose comment un corps peut être uni à un esprit. C'est là le comble de ses difficultés. (Fr. 199)

The turning back upon oneself is complete. The fragment begins as we raise our eyes to the spectacle of Nature's endless extent; that experience ends in bafflement; we look at ourselves, and again encounter paradox, disproportion, mystery.

The theory of proportion and disproportion figures also at the beginning of fragment 418, the wager (actually entitled *"Infini-rien"*). Here God is the sought-for object of knowledge, rather than Nature, but we start with notions drawn from Nature and mathematics.

> Notre âme est jetée dans le corps où elle trouve nombre, temps, dimensions, elle raisonne là-dessus et appelle cela nécessité, et ne peut croire autre chose.

So far so good: a correspondence between knower and known based on number, shape, and time appears to be viable and to lead to knowledge. Then, with the brusque introduction of the *infini*, everything changes. "Le fini s'anéantit en présence de l'infini, et devient un pur néant." That is what happens to the mind, the justice, and the mercy of man, when they are compared to what those terms signify when applied to God. In the improvisatory flow of his thought, Pascal turns next to mathematics. We do know that there is a numerical infinite—an infinite series of numbers—although we do not know its nature: is it odd or even? Three lines later Pascal sums up the whole problem of knowing, when it is conceived as activity that succeeds by proportion or fails (to some degree) by disproportion, in three decisive statements, each of which eliminates in succession a factor present in the preceding.

> Nous connaissons donc l'existence et la nature du fini parce que nous sommes finis et étendus comme lui.
> Nous connaissons l'existence de l'infini et ignorons sa nature, parce que [*var.* nous avons rapport à lui par l'étendue et disproportion avec lui par les limites] il a étendue comme nous, mais non pas des bornes comme nous.
> Mais nous ne connaissons ni l'existence ni la nature de Dieu, parce qu'il n'a ni étendue ni bornes. (Fr. 418)

"Etendue," "bornes," "rapport," "disproportion": note the geometrical vocabulary and, also, the curious correlation of the metaphysical terms "existence" and "nature" with the first two of that group. But the main point is that our approach to God, like our approach to nature, ends in a disproportion. As the factors we share with the objects to be known drop out of the picture, our minds must go blank.

"Incroyable que Dieu s'unisse à nous," writes Pascal at one point in fragment 149 ("A P.-R."). It sums up what we might think at this point regarding the possibility of contact through love and knowledge with God. And yet such union and communication, such *compagnie* and *amitié* (these more concrete words occur in a variant nearby), form the essence of our felicity—intermittently here, eternally in the state of glory. On the face of it, what the humble man might say is right: it is incredible. Pascal finds a way to meet the objection. This humility is false and presumptuous. "L'homme n'est pas digne de Dieu mais il n'est pas incapable d'en être rendu digne" (fr. 239). To overcome the disproportion is something that man cannot do, but God can. "Si on vous unit à Dieu c'est par grâce, non par nature" (fr. 149). By grace, of course, and yet without suppressing nature. In our shadows here below we do effectively see and love something, namely, creatures; we have at least the equipment for that.

> Il est sans doute qu'il connaît au moins qu'il est et qu'il aime quelques choses. Donc s'il voit quelque chose dans les ténèbres où il est et s'il trouve quelque sujet d'amour parmi les choses de la terre, pourquoi si Dieu lui découvre quelque rayon de son essence ne sera-t-il pas capable de la connaître et l'aimer en la manière qu'il lui plaira se communiquer à nous? (Fr. 149)

The disproportion is remedied by a gift from above; the movement from below is met by a movement from above, and specifically by what is necessary for bridging, at least partially, the gap. My point is that Pascal knows what the answer to the problem is from the Bible, but in the old perspective of faith seeking understanding he has his own half-mathematical, half-metaphysical way of interpreting what takes place when the seeker reaches the moment of *pati divina*. For him it is also the moment of certainty.

Conclusion

The experience of certainty is both complex and simple. It can be described in metaphorical language and broken down into intellectual terms. Above all, it is intuitive and immediate. We can see something of this from the ease with which we may diagram it: two terms in opposition, or, when a mediator is added, three terms in harmony; and once the event that can support the latter language has occurred, there is nothing to do except to see and enjoy. If it should happen to us, intervening steps and obstacles would fall away. We would know that Someone is; we would know in some degree what He is or is like; we would feel His presence in us; we would move (or be moved) to perception and possession, the two being inseparably linked. A whole truth and a final good would saturate our powers. Although we know that Pascal distrusts both sense and desire, perhaps the nearest thing to the immediacy and vividness of this experience comes in the life of the senses and in the appetites consequent on their acts. And in fact the imagery of the *Mémorial* is to a significant degree visual, appetitive, and auditive:

> L'an de grâce 1654...lundi 23 novembre.... Depuis environ dix heures et demi du soir jusques environ minuit et demi. Feu... Dereliquerunt me fontem aquae vivae.... Non obliviscar sermones tuos. (Fr. 913)

Sight, thirst, hearing have the quality, when they are satisfied, that Pascal needs in order to express what happened to make his faith certain. The precision as to time reinforces the sense of immediacy; Pascal records the year, the month, the day, and the exact time of that day when the event took place.

This experience of certainty requires divine influence and communication, but it would seem to differ in some respects from two other subjects that interest Pascal very much: prophecy and miracle. Such intervention lies at the source of prophecy. It may lead to prophecy, though not necessarily; and it is plainly not the whole of prophecy, which requires inspired utterance. It has a special relationship to the effect of miracles. In two short sentences Pascal fixes the place of miracles with regard to the other technical elements in his vocabulary.

> Les deux fondements: l'un intérieur, l'autre extérieur, la grâce, les miracles, tous deux surnaturels. (Fr. 861)

> Les miracles prouvent le pouvoir que Dieu a sur les cœurs par celui qu'il exerce sur les corps. (Fr. 903)

The relevance of the fragments concerning miracles to the apologetic part of the *Pensées* is sometimes close, but not always. In the sentences just cited we must say that miracles come into view as means of confirming faith. They are instances in which God makes himself perceptible through the senses rather than through the heart. Elsewhere in fragment 903 Pascal harks back to two Old Testament figures: "Abraham, Gédéon. Confirmer la foi par miracles." Here miracles serve not to produce faith but to promote it. Again, as fragment 861 suggests, by distinguishing external from internal workings of God, miracles fit into a public situation where a doctrine or conviction is being debated and a sign is needed for *discernement*, for discovering where the truth lies. And yet we must not at all downgrade them as elements in Pascal's arsenal. They have their place in the catalogue of proofs: "J'aime mieux suivre. J.-C. qu'aucun autre parce qu'il a le miracle, prophétie, doctrine, perpétuité, etc." (fr. 892).

The fragments concerning miracles, prophecies, and inspiration show us in what final certainty consists. But explanations are not so striking as concrete examples. Given the set of views held by Pascal, it is not surprising that he should be able to furnish such evidence. The experience, if not the records of it, would have to be there to authorize all he has to say about it. And the two documents—not fragments, be it noted—that he did indeed leave us, the *Mémorial* and the *Mystère de Jésus*, were not composed as part of the note-taking for his Apology.[7] They stand behind and above that undertaking, it seems to me. Each of them suggests a triple movement (more obvious in the *Mystère* than in the *Mémorial*, from a meditative beginning to an encounter to a resolution. Of course, the crucial part of the experience is the encounter. It is very remarkable that in both some direct communication, and even exchange, takes place between Pascal and God. In the *Mémorial* it is the God of Abraham, Isaac, and Jacob at first, but as Pas-

cal's experience develops and his record follows his intuitions, Christ moves into the foreground as Redeemer.[8] In
the *Mystère* Christ is the central figure always, though God
as Father is present also. There is never any *doubt* about
what is happening or the validity of it; there is assurance
like that known when persons meet face to face and when
perception is deepened by communication. And what
could be more eloquent than these words from the *Mémorial*: "Certitude, certitude, sentiment, joie, paix." They tell
us compactly, without elaboration, without the distractions of connected speech, what Pascal's goal was and how
strongly he felt about it; they tell us how it is obtained: by
intuition or sentiment; and they name the states that certainty alone can bring. Even so, for all their exemplary
value, these documents do not set down for us the final
paradigm of certainty. What they convey to us is a foretaste
of God as he will be experienced in eternity. Perhaps that is
the shortest way to say what certainty means for Pascal: *the
experience of God, now and hereafter*.

5 | From Certainties to Principles

Toward Certainty in the Pensées

Reason and its activities within its proper realm take up a great deal of the space in the *Pensées*, insofar as the fragments are composed in the context of an Apology.[1] It finds its starting points in common experience and in extensions of common sense. It moves, once in action, along many different lines that suggest or sometimes exemplify distinct methods—geometrical, problematic, dialectical, pragmatic—all designed to yield proofs. The harvest is abundant, as the fragments testify in specific arguments and occasional enumerations. Pascal returns most often to the dialectical mode of thought, beginning with oppositions in things, thoughts, and words, refining them into contradictions, sometimes leaving them to trouble us and make us uncomfortable, at other times—in fact most often—asserting the truth of both sides in some modified form of the original paradox.

What is the final conclusion of this immense intellectual effort? That the Christian religion and the disposition to accept it are not contrary to reason. It is a cautious answer. Exactly what is the degree of certainty that we have reached? This great accumulation of proofs concerning Nature and Scripture ends in something less than conviction. When all is said and done by and to reason, we have made progress, but our state is precarious: it presupposes a complex fabric of discourse. The mobile human mind can still doubt.[2]

Custom, the second of the *moyens de croire* is, precisely, an effective source of stability. The argument centering about custom begins with the conclusions of the preceding stage, which now become opinions (right, perhaps, but that is not yet known) and with the whole person. By habit, nascent beliefs and new patterns of behavior come to pervade the human subject, to work their effects on his powers, and to bring about a moral state that is strongly fixed.

What is the degree and kind of certainty that we attain here in the changes I have just mentioned or in religious beliefs? Clearly we have taken for granted the *évidences* and conclusions—such as they are—of reason, as well as the nature and powers of the human subject. We have taken them for granted and at the same time recognized the need to add something to them to change their quality by basing them on a noncognitive but sure principle of stability. In the area of religion we have not abandoned the first principle, the defensible and defended opinion that the Christian religion is not repugnant to reason. But it has been caught up in the dynamism of the whole person, and there by the force of custom it achieves (in addition to whatever force it had as the conclusion of an elaborate argument) a steadiness and an effectiveness that reason alone cannot attain.

In the last step toward belief, as Pascal turns from the whole creature subject to habit, his thought reverts to inner life and to the heart, which is the decisive place of spiritual ascent. This change in the starting point corresponds to a return from pragmatic reasoning[3] to thought based on the advantages of a dialectical framework and its special power. Of course, everything here is really cumulative; the proofs and habits are present and not forgotten. But they did not bring unshakable conviction; and in the final moment, to the degree that he reasons it out, Pascal falls back on dialectic. I do not mean that he engages in a truly discursive process. At its climax his method tends to become diagrammatic. It can be formulated in an easily grasped schema—two opposed terms, plus a third mediating term—and it serves to give intuited structure to an experience of great tension that is followed by relief, or intense desires to know and possess that are simultaneously satisfied. God is, and He is as He says He is in the Bible—just, merciful, self-giving, redemptive. The prophets knew this kind of inspiration without benefit of reasoning, and now it may come to any seeker with intellectual leanings, like the *honnête homme*, for whom religion must from the beginning make sense.

Something like this conviction occurs in science but only *ex parte subjecti*, for the scientist depends on the heart for his principles; God is not involved. In science there is no inspiration, though I suppose one might speak of a contact with Nature and with things, which reveal themselves under the signs of number, movement, and extension. However, in the domain of religious as distinguished from scientific experience, we have reached the sphere of *évidence* in its supreme sense. We have passed from tentative understanding based on authoritative statements to a meeting with the Author of those statements. The conclusions of reason receive their guarantee; and the force of custom is no longer a blind support of unfounded opinion. Indeed, whereas Pascal likes to dwell on the paradoxical alliance of *le fort* and *le juste* in society, here he can rejoice in the strength that is joined to true knowledge. The last moment of the argument and of the seeker's experience casts its influence back over all that has come before it.

In short, the three phases, the three ways to certain faith

fall into a sequence of mutually assisting parts. Reason takes elements of proof and arranges them in structures or orders designed to move the reader from hostility or nonchalance to a faith-seeking attitude. Custom takes the powers of the reader—or will if he wills—and by repeated acts, the sense of which is implied rather than seen, implants in those powers a habit. Inspiration fills an inner space, perfecting the subject so that his waiting ends in meeting and his estrangement in reconciliation; its essential task is to satisfy innate longings and in so doing to certify itself.

Other Certainties; the General Matrix

I have treated the *Pensées* as a loose ensemble in this study. I am aware of the problems of chronology, of degrees of finish, of destination involved in the text, problems which are unlikely ever to receive wholly convincing solutions. The fragments were written over a period of seven years (1656–62), but the circumstances of composition are only partly known; some received at the hands of Pascal more attention, more correction, more rewriting than others; and, what seems most important of all, they differ in specific aim. There are the texts that Pascal classified in the first twenty-eight *liasses* for the "projet de 1658"; then others that belong to the preparatory phase of that project, such as the series on miracles; others that appear designed to supplement the project or to develop it in some way; still others on the Jesuits and Jansenists that relate to the battle of which the *Provinciales* formed an episode; and finally miscellaneous thoughts and *propos*, some of which might have found their way into the Apology. Through all these differentiations and in all these layers of reflection, one may fairly discern, I think, an overriding aspiration, namely, to tell the truth, the essential mark of which is certainty, and to make statements with such grounds that doubt is removed from the mind.

Because of the thrust noticeable in so many of the fragments, I have emphasized the kind and conditions of certainty involved in religious belief. However, the subject will not stay within those bounds. As noted in discussing proofs and orders, it obliges us to consider the fact that Pascal thinks as a mathematician and a physicist as well as in the manner of a moralist and an apologist. And it is by referring some of our questions to sequences of thought explicit in his other works but only latent in the *Pensées* that we may define better the nature of moral and religious certainty, and at the same time see how a few master themes set the framework for everything else. Given the limits of this book, a few remarks must suffice here.

Coherence and adequacy lead to truth and therefore to certainty: what is said or thought must be consistent and must fit the facts. Pascal does not use those terms, but he might have done so. They name themes that travel from work to work and take on particular colorations according to the category of the work in which they are elaborated. Where the context is strictly mathematical (as in the essay on the *Triangle arithmétique* or in the treatise *Generatio conisectionum*) the facts are present in the form of numbers or figures and coherence is of the axiomatic/deductive sort, for it is based on explicit definitions, statements of assumptions, and a regular technique of demonstration. In a scientific work (like *Nouvelles expériences touchant le vide* or in the *Récit de la grande expérience,* which, though written by Périer, represents a Pascalian mode of thought) the facts are natural phenomena experimentally observed and measured. Truth and certainty arise from sequences discovered in things and reported in a form that approximates the *suite géométrique* of pure mathematics. In a work where the subject matter is moral, as in the *Pensées*, the technical character of the facts is lost: Pascal and his readers are reflecting on experience common to all men, and the type of coherence is primarily dialectical, although traces of axiomatic and empiriometric devices remain, as well as some syllogistic turns at important points. In mathematics and physics Pascal stresses certainty of statement and absence of error; in the domain of morals he stresses certainty of conviction and absence of doubt.

On another level I believe that we may isolate three pairs of notions that are for Pascal metaphysical in their force and application, in the sense that they stand outside any particular problem area or technique of investigation. They establish the matrix within which his reflection tends to occur. The first of these pairs is *fini/infini*. It serves to distinguish and qualify mathematical, natural, and even supernatural objects of knowledge; from these two are derived by specification and combination all possible subject matters. The second pair is *géométrie/finesse*, that is to say, discourse/intuition. It sets up the two essential phases and types of knowing. Both are required, but they may serve as poles, and then characteristic movements of thought assert themselves. One might say that mathematics and physics have their origins in certain principles—such as clearly stated definitions or clearly observed phenomena—and proceed to develop consequences, which are certain, too, by participation, because they depend directly on the prior evidences. Thinking about morals and religion begins, on the other hand, with consequences—the vanities and frustrations of human life—and by an accumulation of convergent limits and proofs comes to a focus on one indubitable principle, God, who confirms, when experienced, all the reasoning activity that has gone before. In mathematics and in nature the discourse may go on without end, and it is at last frustrated by that infinity. In morals and religion the infinite and comprehensive end, though completely out of proportion to us, turns out to be accessible, because it is a Person who makes himself so. *Raison/cœur* is the third pair in this interlocking ensemble of terms. It poses the capacities we need in order to relate ourselves discursively and intuitively to the range of realities in the universe. It also contains a warning for us. In interpreting the *Pensées*, at least, we must not overintellectualize what Pascal cares most about. In the matter of faith there comes a time when reason must submit if it is to receive the One who is the ultimate origin of certainty. The assurance that comes from that meeting can arise only in the heart, as the fruit of an act of knowing and being known that is, equally, an act of loving and being loved.

Notes

Chapter One

1. *Pensées sur la religion et sur quelques autres sujets*, ed. Louis Lafuma (Paris:Editions du Luxembourg, 1952).

2. I do not mean to imply that the *Pensées* are a collection of bits and pieces subject to all sorts of combinations, deconstructions, and reconstructions; but that they are texts of varying length and finish arranged by Pascal into sixty-one groupings, some with explicit titles, some with implicit titles that are more or less clearly discernible. To these, editors customarily add fragments from sources other than the manuscript and the two *Copies*. On this point see the *mises au point* of Jean Mesnard in *Les Pensées de Pascal* (Paris: Sedes, 1976) and the edition prepared by Philippe Sellier (Paris: Mercure de France, 1976). The view of the *Pensées* expressed by Louis Marin in *La Critique du discours* (Paris: Editions de Minuit, 1975) seems excessive. He evokes the image of Pascal cutting pages into smaller bits of text, and he locates as a consequence of that act a "liberté vide" in the work, a "possible du sens" that implies an infinite multiplicity of relationships among the fragments. "En cela le sens échappe à l'auteur qui cesse d'être son générateur pour se livrer à l'aléatoire du commentaire, et d'abord au sien propre dans les arrangements successifs que Pascal imposait à ses

petits papiers ou percevait entre les liasses" (p. 23). Were not the texts more subject to the "aléatoire" before being cut and put in order than after? And, in any case, the "aléatoire" of Pascal's commentary, as expressed in his groupings, would seem to have priority over that of other commentators. Of course Marin is writing a book not on Pascal but on discourse, especially as it is treated by the Port Royalists in their *Logique*. Pascal fits for him, as for Goldmann, into a particular version of *Geistesgeschichte*. In *Le Dieu caché* (Paris: Gallimard, 1955) Goldmann analyzes a "vision du monde," referring it to the *noblesse de robe* and to the coming of dialectical thought; Marin analyzes a conception of language— advanced by Arnauld and Nicole, and in some sense deconstructed by Pascal—referring it as an "index idéologique" to bourgeois mentality and to the coming of the semiological problematic.

3. In his recent edition Philippe Sellier summarizes the contents as follows: "[Les fragments] attestent la diversité des occupations du jeune savant, puisque s'y côtoient de nombreux textes en rapport avec la campagne des *Provinciales*, une note sur le vide, une attaque contre la théologie cartésienne de l'Eucharistie, plusieurs rédactions proches des *Ecrits sur la grâce*, trois dossiers destinés à une *Lettre sur les miracles*, des vestiges de *Discours sur la condition des grands*, des méditations ou des prières.... Néanmoins plus de 80% de ces fragments se rattachent à la préoccupation dominante du Pascal des dernières années, l'élaboration d'une *Apologie de la religion chrétienne*" (p. 7).

4. We gravitate according to temperament and interest toward one or the other of these two poles in our interpretations of Pascal. Some want to track down and clarify the biblical (and related) quotations or allusions. Some want to understand and develop Pascal's acute view of human existence. To the extent that either of these tendencies becomes exclusive, the sense and rhythm of Pascal's thought is lost. He starts with the idea that there are two possible subject matters to which we may address ourselves: Nature and a Book. (I use capital letters here to stress the fact that this is a dichotomy.) Each propounds a thesis—corruption and redemption, respectively; each is a locus of proof supporting its thesis; each complements the other; each is indispensable, logically speaking, to the other. Since these two are exhaustive, we necessarily think in one or the other of the perspectives posed by these realities, but we must give serious attention to both. That of the Book finally subsumes that of Nature, without abolishing it.

5. Lafuma's distinction between "papiers classés" (the first

twenty-seven *liasses* recorded in the *Première Copie* of the fragments) and "papiers non-classés," which was based on the hypothesis of a classification begun but not finished by Pascal, now appears untenable. Jean Mesnard's research has led him to a very different conclusion. "Mais il faut . . . renoncer à l'expression 'papiers non-classés.' On a vu que la seconde partie comportait des unités non moins rigoureusement délimitées que la première et dont beaucoup sont aussi des liasses. L'idée d'un classement interrompu par le fait de circonstances extérieures est indéfendable." See the introduction to his *Les Pensées de Pascal*. The quotation is from p. 29.

6. Cf., however, the opinion of Jean Prigent: "Pascal a donc clairement distingué l'assurance qui vit de la preuve, et *il n'est de bonne preuve que géométrique*; le doute qui naît de l'impuissance à prouver, tout au moins à prouver les principes; la soumission, seule attitude raisonnable de la raison en présence des principes qui dans leur jaillissement et leur être même échappent à son empire." ("Pascal: Pyrrhonien, géomètre, chrétien," in *Pascal présent* [Clermont-Ferrand: Bussac, 1963], pp. 66–67; italics added). All that is true, but from my point of view Prigent fails to distinguish between *démonstration* and *preuve*, and to give to the latter the force it has in texts such as those I am analyzing.

7. In her *The Rhetoric of Pascal* (Amsterdam: Drukkerij Holland N.V. [for Leicester University Press], 1966) Patricia Topliss analyzes at length (pp. 187–238) the arguments in the twenty-seven *liasses* of the Apology. She divides them into two types: "psychological proofs of the only religion that can explain and reconcile man's contradictions" and "historical proofs" of that religion (p. 237). She distinguishes topics and arguments under those two headings and, in an interesting discussion, seeks to arrive at a judgment of the weaknesses and strengths of Pascal's reasoning on each topic. By contrast it is perhaps worth noting that here I am using as data examples of *preuves* (so named by Pascal) and am looking for a classification based on principles that are, as far as possible, intrinsic and constitutive.

8. The attributes Pascal assigns par excellence to the Christian religion are indicated by the adjectives "vraie" and "aimable." His Apology stands or falls according to the value of the proofs he finds to justify them.

9. See "Conflict and Resolution in Pascal's *Pensées*," *Romanic Review* 49 (1958): 12–24, and also *Audience, Words, and Art* (Columbus: Ohio State University Press, 1965), pp. 134–40.

10. To recapture the exact tenor of the fragment we must doubt-

less conceive first a finite nature (that of man) facing physical Nature, which is doubly infinite—hence the "disproportion de l'homme"—and then the consequence of that dissimilarity, which is a weakness, an inability, and specifically, an inability to know. It is interesting to see that Pascal apparently intended originally to entitle his reflections "Incapacité de l'homme." But, as the variant shows, he turned from the effect to the reason or cause, from the state of human powers to something more fundamental, differences in kinds of being.

11. For an excellent discussion of authority as it applies to the Bible, to the prophets, and to God, see André Gounelle, *La Bible selon Pascal* (Paris: Presses universitaires de France, 1970), especially pp. 7–26.

12. The following schema presents the distinctions according to which I have classified Pascal's proofs. I have added to the right the aspects of human nature to which the various proofs are directed. Naturally such a table calls for qualifications, particularly as regards the interacting and overlapping functions of mind, heart, and body; some *nuances*, at least, are noted in chapters 2 and 3.

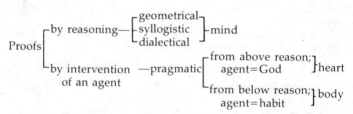

13. Henri Gouhier draws attention to the importance of this text in his study of the genesis of the Apology. See *Blaise Pascal: Commentaires* (Paris: Vrin, 1971), pp. 172–73. He assumes (rightly, I think) behind these items a line of thought going back to the project of a letter on miracles, while the treatment of man's fate apart from God is prefigured in the *Entretien avec M. de Sacy*. Pascal's Apology as we have it results thus from joining and elaborating partially two groups of apologetic reflections.

Chapter Two

1. See the first *liasse*, "Ordre," and also fragments 298, 427, 467, 512, 620, 683, 684, 694, 696, 733.

2. Pascal treats the kinds of order (in the sense of domain) as radically separate from each other. He tends to do the same thing

in discussing order (as sequence). When he turns to the latter, we note parallel consequences. Just as we cannot get thought out of a body or charity out of thought, so we cannot get the order of the heart out of the procedures of geometry. See the excellent remarks on this point by J. Russier in *Blaise Pascal: l'homme et l'oeuvre* (Paris: Editions de minuit, 1956), pp. 234–35.

3. Thus the Pyrrhonian "order" of completely spontaneous and unreflective expression would seem to lie near but at one remove from judgments made according to *finesse*.

4. The decision to use these two terms as I have in analyzing the *Pensées* raises complicated questions that cannot be discussed at length here. I assume the following: (1) that in intellectual history "rhetoric" and "dialectic" have been used in many different and often opposed senses; (2) that the two functions involved—communicating and reasoning—are interrelated; (3) that any writer of first rank has his own way of defining and relating the two terms or their synonyms; and (4) that Pascal has his way of doing so. It is interesting to see what happens when these assumptions are not operative. One may, for example, take as a point of departure "traditional rhetoric," understood as a comprehensive and independent technique of expression; then dialectic gets short shrift, and Pascal becomes a Ciceronian *malgré lui*, as in *The Rhetoric of Pascal* by Patricia Topliss. Or again one may take as a point of departure dialectic, understood as a comprehensive and independent technique or inquiry; then rhetoric is neglected, and Pascal becomes a precursor of Hegel and Marx, as in Lucien Goldmann's *Le Dieu caché*. Each of these authors has important things to say about the *Pensées*, but the peculiarities of Pascal's rhetoric and dialectic seem to elude them. For a view closer to mine, see E. Morot-Sir, *La métaphysique de Pascal* (Paris: Presses universitaires de France, 1973), chap. 1 and passim.

5. Here I am not trying to recover the plan of the Apology or the logic of the first twenty-seven *liasses*, but to define and extend the notion of sequence stated or implied in certain fragments notable for their comprehensive character. Cf. the view of Jean Orcibal, who comments on the tendency to reduce "Infini-rien" to mathematical formulas instead of studying the fragment as a whole and then putting it in a larger context. He concludes: "Ainsi donc, malgré son mode invraisemblable de composition, le fragment *Infini-rien* range selon une progression très nette les étapes qui conduisent de l'athéisme négateur au seuil de la foi et il fait allusion à un si grand nombre d'entre elles qu'on peut le considérer comme un abrégé de presque toute l'Apologie." (*Blaise Pascal: l'homme et l'oeuvre*, p. 174.) If one concentrates too much on stat-

ing the terms of the wager or on determining its place in the Apology, one may overlook the outline of conversion it contains. What may be seen in "Infini-rien" reappears on a more abstract level in fragment 808 (concerning the *moyens de croire*) the systematic implications of which I am working out in this book.

6. To me it seems important to stress the real intellectual progress—as Pascal sees the matter—that occurs in the demonstrative section of the wager. The mind grasps something it did not understand before, namely, that the attitude of belief is rationally defensible. Cf., however, the phraseology of Jean Mesnard (in *Pascal* [Desclée de Brouwer, 1965]): "L'homme ne peut atteindre Dieu par ses seules forces. La raison le démontre; la religion le suppose. Pourtant l'homme n'est pas condamné à *l'irrationel du pari*" (p. 45). A few lines further on he continues: "L'esprit, *qui demeurait aveugle* quand la volonté se trouvait placée devant l'exigence contraignante du pari, est pénétrée d'une lumière nouvelle." (All italics added.)

7. I am emphasizing the intellectual aspects of Pascal's dialectic. For an illuminating discussion of its imaginative underpinnings, see the sections on "les schèmes imaginatifs du sentiment" of Pascal in Louis Marin's *La Critique du discours*, pp. 400–412.

8. The role of dogmatists and Pyrrhonians, Stoics and Epicureans, Epictetus and Montaigne in the *Pensées* reveals clearly the special way in which Pascal understands the history of ideas and the history of philosophy. He has little feeling for or interest in the objective scope, balance, and adequacy of philosophical thought. Cf. the following remark of Henri Gouhier: "Il faut bien voir ici ce qui devait apparaître nouveau et important à l'apologiste dans sa façon d'utiliser les philosophes. . . . Il ne s'agit pas d'une recherche de la vérité avec une zone de vérités rationelles à traverser avant d'entrer dans celle des vérités de foi: il s'agit d'une préparation à la conversion en créant une situation propice à l'action de la grâce s'il plaît à Dieu de l'envoyer." (*Blaise Pascal: Commentaires* [Paris: Vrin, 1971], p. 97.) I agree with this conclusion, but perhaps it is worth adding that there is some truth in what Pascal's philosophers say. In their theses and antitheses they are repeating what can already be seen on the level of common sense and experience, namely, that man and human nature are the subjects of contradictory predicates. Philosophers do not state truths directly; they bear witness to the diverse sides of an integral truth that exceeds their powers. Pascal operates on their works something exactly analogous to his figurative interpretation of the Old Testament.

9. "Powers" in the plural, necessarily, because of the radical separation of the orders to which they address themselves.

10. Because of Pascal's antimetaphysical bias, what is eventually known will depend on empiriometrical investigation and not on inquiry into essences.

11. In *Pascal savant et croyant* (Paris: Presses universitaires, 1957), Georges Leroy, noting the similar rhythms of Pascal's procedures in the domains of science and religion, makes a valuable distinction between "idées claires" and "idées éclairantes." In general he finds that Descartes strives for the former, whereas Pascal seeks the latter. That seems true where the intuitive bases of science or religion are concerned: Pascal moves up his scale to locate explanatory ideas or *principes*. However, in the discursive phase of his mathematical and physical treatises, does he not insist on fixed definitions and the *idées claires* that go into them? Cf. also the passages on demonstration in "De l'Esprit géométrique et de l'art de persuader," pp. 349 and 356–67 in the *Oeuvres complètes* as edited by Louis Lafuma (in the series "L'Intégrale" [Paris: Editions du seuil, 1963]).

12. See above, p. 44.

13. A good example of such confusions, one that was well known to Pascal, is the attribution to Nature of an *horreur du vide*.

14. Note that factors (2) and (3) may have the same or similar traits: the proper role of both is to evolve toward the model delineated by (1).

15. The framework that Pascal chooses reminds one of the situation used by Diderot in the *Neveu de Rameau*. Perhaps it has not been sufficiently stressed that *Moi* and *Lui*, who have parts to play in the social pantomime, withdraw from the game, putting physical and intellectual distance between it and them for enough time to air and sift judgments that bear (1) on society, art, and morals and (2) on their particular relationship to those things.

16. Duvignaud comes very close to my view in some penetrating remarks reported on pp. 293–94 of *Blaise Pascal: l'homme et l'oeuvre*. But I prefer not to go so far as he does in the following lines: "On peut se demander s'il ne faudrait pas chercher dans Pascal le rhétoricien, l'homme de persuasion, l'homme chez qui la communication précède l'ontologie—une psychologie pascalienne devrait sans doute fonder la métaphysique pascalienne sur une étude des moyens de toucher et de vaincre" (p. 294). The problem he treats, the relation of communication to ontology and metaphysics, is almost identical to my concern with the relation of rhetoric to dialectic. To decide which "precedes" the other one

must decide whether one wishes to think in terms of priority in time or in nature. If one chooses the second kind of priority, as I do here, one must say, it seems to me, that just as God precedes man, so the discovery of the truth about God precedes communicating it. See above, note 4.

Chapter Three

1. I have called Pascal a dualist more than once in these pages. One might justly say, however, that the term is inadequate or needs to be understood in a special way. A third principle or reality is almost constantly present in the *Pensées: charité, sainteté, divinité*. Whenever Pascal leaves behind the context of natural psychology, this third principle asserts itself.

2. On the dualism of man and on my assimilation of the terms "machine," "automate," and "corps" to each other, cf. E. Gilson's essay "Pascal et l'abêtissement" in *Les Idées et les lettres* (Paris: Vrin, 1932), especially pp. 269–70. Since he is commenting on Pascal's use of *abêtir*, he adds "bête" and "animal" to this string of synonyms and near-synonyms.

3. To measure the extraordinary equivocation on the word "cœur" as one looks back from Pascal to Descartes, see the *Discours de la méthode, 5ᵉ partie*, pp. 157–63, and the *Traité des passions, pt. 1, arts*. 7–10, pp. 697–700, in the Bibliothèque de la Pléiade volume, *Descartes: Oeuvres et lettres*, ed. André Bridoux (Paris: Gallimard, 1953).

4. The arithmetic machine outdoes animals in "thought"; animals outdo the machine in "willing"—indeed, there is nothing comparable to will in the machine. Pascal does not mention man here or otherwise develop his argument. But are we not on the verge of a variation on the theme of the three orders? He refers to *machine* (=*corps*), *pensée*, and *volonté*, and he touches on the problem of the distinction between the orders. We can get something like thought out of a body, after all; and animals have something like thought and will. In men body, thought, and will may be so clearly distinguished as to give orders infinitely distant from each other. I take this fragment as further evidence of Pascal's habit of using—in the *Pensées*—his technical vocabulary in an analogical way. He delights in differentiating, grading, and assimilating.

5. Every proportion implies some variation as it moves from one application to another.

6. Regarding the sequence of ideas from demonstration and the role of reason to action and the role of custom, which seems to

result from an associative link in Pascal's mind, see the useful remarks, based on manuscript evidence, that Georges Brunet proposes in *Le Pari de Pascal* (Paris: Desclée de Brouwer, 1956), pp. 97–99.

7. On this order of events Léon Brunschvicg has a different and, I believe, very debatable view. Cf. the following passage: "Comme on l'a vu par les Fragments qui terminent la Section précédente, ce sont les passions qui empêchent l'intelligence du libertin de pénétrer les vérités de la foi. Une fois les passions vaincues par la discipline à laquelle l'Eglise soumet la machine, il sera possible à la raison de se convaincre que tout au moins la Religion n'est pas contre la raison, et les obstacles sont ôtés qui venaient de la passion ou de l'intelligence; la voie est préparée au sentiment." (From Brunschvicg's edition of the *Pensées et opuscules* [Paris: Hachette, n.d.], p. 448, note 2.) Instead of *raison, coutume, inspiration* operating as factors in that order (my view), he sees a movement from *machine* to *intelligence* to *sentiment*. We are obviously talking about the same means of belief. But it seems to me more accurate to say that the passions, rather than hindering the intelligence in understanding the truths of faith, corrupt the will and turn it from the true Good toward lesser goods. With that in mind, it is proper to say that Pascal's order is (1) to ask and answer questions raised by and for the mind, (2) to recommend the means of appeasing and redirecting the passions, and (3) to promote a state in which inspiration or *sentiment* is awaited. The interactions of these factors are such that one should avoid mechanical separations and sequences. Still, Brunschvicg's analysis appears unfaithful to the letter and to the logical trend, indicated more than once, of Pascal's thought.

8. On the side of reason Pascal cannot produce a demonstration, that is, a carefully articulated body of doctrine. He cannot, because of what God and men are. But he may move his reader toward a new habit of mind. A habit is formed by repeated acts. Pascal can exhibit to him, instance by instance, the multitude of proofs that support Christianity; the cumulative effect of these acts of understanding may not be certainty, but it is a definite and positive attitude.

9. At all times a third person is more or less obscurely present to the discourse, the apologist, and the reader. No stage of conversion is entirely apart from God. Both the original indifference and the intermediate seeking are defined relative to Him, to say nothing of the final inspiration. To the *chercheur* we may surely apply the "Tu ne me chercherais pas si tu ne m'avais trouvé."

Chapter Four

1. In reconstructing the seeker's path one may evoke once more the "Tu ne me chercherais pas..." It throws light on the whole moral evolution that occurs on the way to conversion. The *recherche* itself is defined by a lack that has a particular character, a lack that forecasts the end to be found and is determined by that end. The end is present by implication in the itinerary. Thus we underline once more the fundamental unity of the apologetic argument. Even Pascal's *preuves par la nature*, associated with the beginning of the search, presuppose a particular idea of nature—of human nature (to be specific) in a fallen state. But whoever accepts that concept has in so doing taken for granted half of what is to be proved. For further comment on this point, see the concluding lines of Th. Spoerri's paper, "Les Pensées de derrière la tête de Pascal." in *Pascal: l'homme et l'oeuvre*.

2. My retrospective procedure here resembles somewhat that of Pascal as he reasons backward to the explanation of what happened to produce the "dispossessed king." But this movement is only episodic; the true direction for man cannot point into himself. Cf. Saint Augustine, *Confessions*, 1.1.1: "...fecisti nos ad te et inquietum est cor nostrum donec requiescat in te."

3. What is involved here is primarily an experience, a contact, a fulfilment, and not an act or state of contemplation. Cf. Jean Mesnard's remark concerning Pascal and the love of truth: "L'amour de la vérité, tel que le conçoit Pascal, n'est pas caractérisé par une attitude de contemplation, de possession de la vérité trouvée, mais une attitude de recherche d'une vérité inconnue et désirée. L'amour s'allie donc, ici encore, à une sorte d'insatisfaction, un sentiment d'un vide à remplir. Ce vide, seul Dieu, vérité absolue, a pouvoir de le combler." (*Pascal* [n.p., Desclée de Brouwer, 1964], p. 78).

4. See above, chapter 1 pp. 17–18.

5. That Pascal considers the role of God in human history to be absolutely evident—even though He is a hidden God—serves to pinpoint the serious limitations of the views expressed by Lucien Goldmann in *Le Dieu caché*. The fact is inexplicable, but the positive phase of Pascal's dialectic seems to have escaped Goldmann's attention. He insists that *croire* and *parier* are one and the same, in line with his excessive stress on God's transcendence, and thereby throws Pascal's position irremediably off-balance. As a further consequence he arrives at a "vision tragique" for Pascal that does not fit the textual data. Jean Mes-

nard's formulation of the problem in terms of "ironie," "tragique," and "mystique" manages to save the genuinely valuable features of Goldmann's interpretation for those who want to understand Pascal but remain unconvinced by the history of ideas and methods developed in *Le Dieu caché*. See Mesnard, *Les Pensées de Pascal* (Paris: SEDES, 1976), pt. 3, "La Signification des Pensées*.

6. In a sense the establishment of proportions or the remedying of disproportions is only a preliminary. After that, what? Pascal writes in the conclusion to the *Traité de l'équilibre des liqueurs*: "Les expériences sont les véritables maîtres qu'il faut suivre dans la physique." I find it suggestive, though paradoxical and finally unsatisfactory, to extend this principle as follows. Experiments require an hypothesis of some kind, a way of thinking and acting *as if* so-and-so were the case, which is then confirmed or contradicted by direct contact with the subject matter being studied. We think and act *as if* the lightest and heaviest liquids (air and mercury) are in an equilibrium, and when we adopt the right set of interrogative procedures Nature will say *yes* or *no*, and if the former, the *as if* is removed, and the principles and reasonings are taken as demonstrated. But we encounter the same device in apologetics. The fragment "Infini-rien" uses it in two forms. There is an intellectual *as if* coming at the end of the wager, and a moral *as if* adopted later by the seeker when he accepts the advice to "s'abêtir." The resulting hypothetical mode of thought and action prepares us for another *yes* or *no*, this time reaching us not on the initiative of Nature but on that of God. And so we approach truth "experimentally" in both physics and religion. Even geometry has an *as if* in its undefined and undefinable starting points; and Nature (as quantity) confirms them. Mathematics is not for Pascal purely a matter of freely chosen conventions, as it tends to be for us. He considers it to be a science that tells the truth about something, and under certain conditions that something will confirm what is said about it. I fear, however, that the force of this reductive approach to Pascal's methods rests on an illusion created by overindulgence in analogies.

7. Regarding the probable occasion and the date of the "Mystère," see the recent Sellier edition of the *Pensées*, p. 442, n. 25, and Louis Lafuma's note in his edition of 1951, 3:178.

8. It is easier to trace the phases of the experience recorded in the *Mémorial* than to fix the sense of what happened. In general I agree with the analyses proposed by Henri Gouhier in *Blaise Pascal: Commentaires*, pp. 42–49. Pascal does not pass from ignorance

to knowledge but undergoes a felt guarantee of what he already knew without effective conviction. He becomes certain of the world's vanity, of God's accessibility, of an available Redeemer. He does not receive assurance of his own *élection*: that is not certain, for separation and abandonment are still possible. As Gouhier says (p. 47): "C'est une certitude, mais qu'obsède la crainte, une joie mais dont le frémissement est tremblement." Thus it is important always to distinguish between such an encounter and beatitude. However, in deciding whether one may speak or not of a "mystical experience" apropos of the *Mémorial*, Gouhier defines that phrase too narrowly, in my opinion, and comes to debatable negative conclusions.

Chapter Five

1. Throughout the chapters of this book I have intended to describe and treat the processes of intellectual invention—without, however, neglecting the importance of *sentiment*—found in the *Pensées* and within the context just noted. For an illuminating general essay on the subject of invention in the works of Pascal and an attempt to state in concrete terms the originality of Pascal, cf. Jean Mesnard, "L'Invention chez Pascal," in *Pascal présent*, pp. 41–58.

2. Jean Prigent warns: "L'on ne souligne pas assez l'acharnement de Pascal à reconnaître, à proclamer, quand il recommande cet examen [des preuves du christianisme], les droits de la raison" (*Pascal présent*, p. 69). We may well agree with Prigent and with Pascal, whom he quotes pertinently from fragment 505 ("C'est le consentement de vous à vous-même, et la voix constante de votre raison et non des autres, qui vous doit faire croire"), and also with God, whom Pascal feigns to quote in fragment 149 ("Je n'entends pas que vous soumettiez votre créance à moi sans raison"), and nonetheless find some distortion in the view expressed by Prigent. There are still three means of belief, and Pascal shows "acharnement" in treating all of them and in cutting one of them—reason—down to size.

3. "Pragmatic" because it seeks and finds an effective means for accomplishing an end.

Index